Schooling as Violence

This book asks fundamental questions about the nature and purposes of formal education. There are three main ways of looking at the relationship between formal education, individuals and society:

- that education improves society;
- that education reproduces society exactly as it is;
- that education makes society worse and harms individuals.

Whilst much academic writing and research stresses the first two functions, the third is largely played down or ignored.

In this unique, thought-provoking book, **Clive Harber** argues that while schooling can play a positive role, violence towards children originating in the school's system is common, systematic and widespread, and that schools play a significant role in encouraging violence in wider society. Topics covered include physical punishment, learning to hate others, sexual abuse, stress and anxiety and the militarisation of school.

It should be read by anyone involved in education – from students and academics to policy makers and practitioners around the world.

Clive Harber is Professor of International Education and Head of the School of Education at the University of Birmingham.

Schooling as Violence
How schools harm pupils and societies

Clive Harber

RoutledgeFalmer
Taylor & Francis Group

LONDON AND NEW YORK

First published 2004 by RoutledgeFalmer
2 Park Square, Milton Park, Abingdon, Oxon OX14 4RN

Simultaneously published in the USA and Canada
by RoutledgeFalmer
29 West 35th Street, New York, NY 10001

RoutledgeFalmer is an imprint of the Taylor & Francis Group

© 2004 Clive Harber

Typeset in Sabon by BC Typesetting Ltd
Printed and bound in Great Britain by
TJ International Ltd, Padstow, Cornwall

British Library Cataloguing in Publication Data
A catalogue record for this book is available from the British Library

Library of Congress Cataloging in Publication Data
A catalog record for this book has been requested

ISBN 0–415–34434–4 (pbk)
ISBN 0–415–34433–6 (hbk)

Contents

Introduction

> . . . it is both intriguing and depressing to note that while the finest minds
> engaged themselves in the long struggle for universal basic education, once
> provision as such was universalised many of them lost interest in what was
> provided
>
> (Alexander 2000: 172)

I should not be in a position to write this book. Education and learning as
manifested in formal schooling should be, and is usually taken to be,
obviously and consistently good for pupils. However, the sad truth is that
formal, mass education – schooling – cannot automatically be linked with
enlightenment, progress and liberty and indeed too often can be linked to
pain and suffering. Those who have read the works of writers such as
Illich (1971), Nyerere (1967), Freire (1972), Postman and Weingartner
(1969) and Holt (1969) that came out of educational debates of the late
1960s and early 1970s will be familiar with the argument that all too
often the hallmarks of conventional schooling are authoritarianism, boredom, irrelevance, frustration and alienation. These were and are important
arguments that influenced the present writer. However, this book differs
from these previous works in a number of important respects. First, the
central argument of this book is that the situation is too often actually
worse than the one portrayed in these now classic texts in that formal
schooling has often been directly violent both to learners and to the wider
society. Overwhelmingly educational debates globally concentrate either
on *access* (e.g. Education For All) and/or on the *positive* outcomes of
schooling. There is also some recognition of the role of schooling in *reproducing* social, economic and political inequality, including certain forms of
violence, though this is less common. While these perspectives are important
and have much truth in them, what is usually ignored or not admitted is
that schools are often violent towards children and directly involved in the
active *perpetration* of violence in the wider society. Reference in the press
to violence in schools is most commonly about pupil to teacher or pupil to
pupil violence. While this is often very distressing and unpleasant for those

involved, rarely is the role of the school itself seen as problematic in any systematic way. The present book does not claim to be balanced in itself in that it concentrates on the violence done to learners in schools, but it does help to balance debates about the relationships between schooling and the wider society. Second, this book is consciously international in its attempt to analyse formal schooling as a globally problematic phenomenon. Third, while the book argues a case, it is not a polemical work because the argument is based wherever possible on existing academic work and empirical evidence. A fourth point is that since the late 1960s we have managed to accumulate not only a wide range of studies that illuminate the negative side of schooling but also a range of studies that suggest how education can be more positively organised along democratic lines.

The arguments and evidence provided in the book are unsettling and disturbing and are intended to challenge orthodoxies because these are issues that need to be openly confronted and discussed if formal education is to play a less negative role in the future. However, it must be stressed at the outset, though the point will be addressed again later, that the purpose of this book is very definitely not to criticise teachers or teaching as a profession. I was a teacher, a number of my in-laws are teachers and quite a number of close friends are teachers, so I understand the realities of teaching. The book is concerned with schooling as a historical, social and political *system* that shapes and influences the behaviour of individuals. It is true that important aspects of educational systems need to be changed to encourage different forms of behaviour, as the book makes clear, but blaming individuals or the profession is not the aim of the book.

It is, of course, also the case that schooling is not the sole socialisation agency responsible for contributing to violence. The family and the mass media, for example, also have a role to play. However, while reference is made to other socialisation agencies, each of these would require a book in their own right and here the focus is on formal schooling.

Underlying the book is a strong personal commitment to democracy as a political system, both at the macro level and at the level of institutions and individual behaviour, and to the importance of education for democracy. This is discussed in various places in the book but especially in Chapter 10 where case studies of education for democracy are reviewed. The global struggle for democracy and human rights is complex and difficult and has not necessarily been helped by recent attempts to impose it by military force on other countries. Despite a certain amount of bad press for democracy, however, it remains the worst form of government – apart from all the others, as Winston Churchill once put it, and education for, in and about democracy is the key to combating the ills discussed in this book.

I have long had an interest in the relationships between education and politics but violence and the contexts that give rise to violence have consistently played a part in my research and personal experience. Research carried out in Nigeria in the late 1970s confirmed the authoritarian nature of colonially inherited schooling, including the use of corporal punishment, and caused me to reflect on the nature of schooling provided in the UK where I had recently been a teacher in a large state comprehensive school, during a period when corporal punishment was still used in schools. Research work on colonial education systems and resistance to them in Kenya, Tanzania, Zimbabwe, Namibia, Eritrea and South Africa reinforced this nascent interest in education and violence, especially in the last four cases where schools were the site of violent military oppression and violent resistance (Harber 1989, 1997a). Research and writing on political education for democracy, on the other hand (e.g. Harber 1987; Harber and Meighan 1989; Harber 1996; Harber and Davies 1997) was connected both in the sense of suggesting the dominant position of authoritarian forms of schooling globally but also the potential for more democratic forms of education to reduce levels of violence. This interest really crystallized, however, around the notion of schooling as violence, towards the end of a period of living and working in South Africa between 1995 and 1999. South Africa is a very violent society and South African schools are plagued by violence (Harber 2001a), as a number of sections of this book will illustrate, and I carried out research on a non-governmental organisation involved in violence reduction in schools (Harber 2001b). Again, research on one particular school engaged in a process of transformation also suggested that more democratic forms of organisation could reduce levels of hate and conflict, in this case based on racism (Harber 1998a). However, the more I read and reflected on schooling and violence and connected it to earlier work on the political nature of schooling, the more I became convinced that schooling itself was often responsible both for initiating violence and for reproducing and perpetrating forms of violence existing in the wider society. The more I looked the more I found instances and examples of schooling having a violent impact on learners. However, each instance seemed to be regarded as an aberration – a one-off peculiarity – or schooling's role in perpetrating violence was analysed in relation to one particular theme such as gender or race. There didn't seem to be an attempt to link themes and instances to suggest that this situation was not accidental or based on chance but was caused by the very nature of schooling itself. This book sets out to explore this argument, the evidence that gives rise to it and the underlying reasons why schooling is implicated in violence.

Note: Use of the terms 'development', 'developing country' and 'developed country' in the text are not regarded as unproblematic, even though it is not the purpose of this book to explore them systematically. Readers who are interested in these debates should see Fagerlind and Saha (1989) and Harber and Davies (1997).

1 Is formal education always good for you?

Schoolchildren, teachers and teaching union representatives legged it to Downing Street last week to present Tony Blair with a book to highlight the lack of free education around the world. It contains letters and pictures written and drawn by children in England and Africa to show why education is an important right . . . Chris Keates, deputy general secretary of the teaching union NASUWT, said: 'It's important for children in this country to avoid taking for granted the education to which they are entitled. Although they might complain about school, at least they have the right to be there. This is not the case for an estimated 125 million people worldwide'. Try telling that to the 50,000 truants every day whom the government wants to catch in a fresh burst of 'sweeps' next month.

(*Education Guardian* 30/4/2002)

The impact of violent conflict on schooling

Schooling internationally takes place in many different contexts and violence is certainly one of them (Harber and Davies 1997: Ch. 1). In 2000 1.6 million people worldwide died as a result of self-inflicted, interpersonal or collective violence (WHO 2002: 9). War and violent conflict are universally seen as bad for socio-economic and political development and one reason is the effect that war and violence has on young people and their education. As UNICEF recently put it,

In the armed conflicts of recent years children have been not only unintended victims but deliberate targets of violence. The number of children who have been directly affected is enormous. Millions of them have been killed, disabled, orphaned, sexually exploited and abused, abducted and recruited as soldiers, uprooted from their homes, separated from their families and faced with heightened risk of disease and malnutrition.

(UNICEF 2001: 1)

A casual glance at a world atlas brings home the wide range of countries where such conflicts have recently taken place – Afghanistan, Albania, Bosnia, Chechnya, Colombia, the Democratic Republic of the Congo, Guatemala, Kosovo, India, Indonesia, Iraq, Israel, Nepal, Northern Ireland, Palestine, Philippines, Rwanda, Sierra Leone, Somalia, Sri Lanka, Sudan, Turkey, Uganda, Zimbabwe and so on.

Such conflicts have regularly directly affected the provision of schooling and in such circumstances pupils are not necessarily safe at school. Examples could be found from most of the above countries but the following four extracts from articles in the *Times Educational Supplement* provide graphic illustration of the impact that violent conflict has on schools.

Nepal

After a brutal week in which teachers and schools have endured bombs, murder and kidnap by Maoists, a British-run charity is launching a human rights education . . . Maoists have been accused of recruiting child soldiers, abduction, torture and murder while the police have been accused of killing civilians suspected of Maoists activities. Last week, in the remote area of Gorka, the headteacher of a village school was taken from his bed and hacked to death by insurgents . . . In Jumla, Nepalese Teachers Association President Ishwori Datta Neupane, who is also a head, was abducted from his home after refusing to make a donation of NRS 80,000 (£800) to Maoist rebels. A few nights earlier, school buses belonging to the Modern Indian School in Kathmandu were destroyed by bombs . . . A bomb hurled at Vishwa Gorkha Academy made a one-metre hole in the wall of the school on the outskirts of the city.

(Wiggs 2000)

Turkey

About 4,000 villages in the south-east, where 90% of people are Kurdish, were forcibly evacuated by the security forces as part of the counter-insurgency campaign. Many villages were also burnt to the ground. With the resultant migration to the cities and no investment in new schools, in 15 years, class sizes have shot up. 'We have 150 primary and secondary schools in the Diyarbakir region for 173,000 kids. That's about 80 to a classroom', said Figen Aras, the union secretary and a high-school teacher. 'How can they get an education this way?' Within this traditional society of south-eastern Turkey, a collapse in the education system hits female students hardest. 'We estimate that that about 30% of boys and 60% of girls don't get any education', said Mr. Aras.

(Gorvett 2000)

Chechnya

According to Ramzan Avtorkhanov (a school director at a tented camp for refugees), there has been virtually no education system in Chechnya for five or six years. The present generation of children and adolescents has grown up amid the violence, wreckage and poverty of conflict with no schooling. When the first round of fighting ended in 1996, many schools, especially those in villages, did not re-open.

(Brooks 2000)

Zimbabwe

More than 2,000 teachers were assaulted and at least one was murdered in Zimbabwe during the run-up to the nation's elections last weekend. Government militia targeted teachers as part of their months long campaign of terror against all opposition supporters . . . The Progressive Teachers Union of Zimbabwe said that more than 9,000 teachers and 551 schools had been affected by the Mugabe-led wave of political violence and 2096 teachers had been assaulted. It also received reports of 12 teachers or their wives being raped and 25 pupils being abducted or raped by Zanu-PF thugs.

(MacGregor 2000)

Furthermore, in Zimbabwe, in the midst of serious food shortages, Mr Mugabe's Deputy Foreign Minister said that anyone who voted for the opposition could not expect to get food aid from the government and the self-styled war veterans have enforced this by deliberately stopping the distribution of food to schoolchildren in areas where their parents have supported the opposition in elections (Black 2002; Meldrum 2002).

The negative impact of these types of violent conflict on schooling is universally regarded as especially serious not only because of the obvious physical and psychological harm done to the pupils and teachers concerned but also because schooling as an institution is normally seen as inherently beneficial to society because it is a key agency of human development. But is this necessarily so?

Is formal education good for development?

The children learn nothing that is of use to them in that school. All the teachers do is to stop them from doing useful work. There is not enough water in the village and it has to be brought in. It takes three hours to walk to their fields and they often have to stay overnight. They cannot leave their children in the village. Who would look after them? The teachers? Once, long ago, the old man recalls, his grandson came home and showed him how to make compost. That was the only time either of them had profited from school.

(Zimmer 1992: 240, recounting discussions in a Mong village in
northern Thailand)

Every year the United Nations Development Programme (UNDP) produces a book called the *Human Development Report*. This is perhaps the most authoritative international statement on issues surrounding human development. In this annual publication the UNDP ranks all the countries of the world from 1 to 162 according to a wide range of variables, but special emphasis is laid on what they term the 'Human Development Index'. This is a composite index of what they consider to be the four key indicators of human development. These are life expectancy at birth, the adult literacy rate, wealth per capita and, most important for present purposes, the combined enrolment rates for primary, secondary and tertiary levels of formal education. Thus it is assumed that enrolment in formal education is necessarily and inherently a 'good thing', that it is a key indicator of development and that what happens inside schools and higher education is automatically of benefit to both individuals and society. This assumption is shared, most of the time, by national governments, global institutions like the World Bank and international aid agencies where the dominant concern is with access to schooling rather than what happens in schooling. This is reflected in the enormous global expenditure on formal education and the major conference held at Jomtien, Thailand in 1990 when most governments of the world met to plan how they would provide universal primary education for all children by the year 2000 – followed by a similar enormous conference held in Dakar, Senegal in 2000 where they met again to explain why they hadn't achieved their targets for 2000 but would do so by 2015. Globally, there is far more concern with rights *to* education than rights *in* education because formal education is perceived in an overwhelmingly positive light. An example of this is UNESCO's publication *Education for All: Is the World on Track?* (UNESCO 2002). This is the report of the team set up to monitor global progress in Education For All since Dakar. This portrays education (largely interpreted as schooling) as an undisputedly and unproblematically good thing, even claiming that,

> education is also an indispensable means of unlocking and protecting other human rights by providing the scaffolding that is required to secure good health, liberty, security, economic well-being and participation in social and political activity. Where the right to education is guaranteed, people's access to and enjoyment of other rights is guaranteed.
> (UNESCO 2002: 14)

Yet in reality education is paradoxical in that under the general rubric of 'education' many good things take place but many bad things (as well as many indifferent things) take place as well. Despite the global emphasis on access to education described above, there is nothing inherently good about education, schooling or learning. Learning can either be very good or very bad depending on what is learnt, how it is learnt and what it is designed to do. This is a quotation from a teacher which captures this dual potential well,

> I have come to a frightening conclusion: I am the decisive element in the classroom. It is my personal approach that creates the climate. It is my daily mood that makes the weather. As a teacher I possess tremendous power to make a child's life miserable or joyous. I can be a tool of torture or an instrument of inspiration. I can humiliate, humour, hurt or heal. In all situations it is my response that decides whether a crisis will be escalated or de-escalated, and a child humanised or dehumanised.
>
> (Ginott 1972: 15–16)

The bulk of this book explores ways in which formal schooling has often been harmful to children and their wider societies in the form of both being violent and helping to reproduce and perpetrate violence. However, even though schooling may not necessarily do anything directly violent or harmful, it often doesn't do anything positive for pupils or their families either. As a result there are significant levels of rejection of formal schooling globally and this rejection can be for good reasons as well as bad. It is certainly not always based on blind ignorance or irrationality. Low levels of school enrolment are common in developing countries and a particular problem is that of retention – keeping pupils in school once they have been sent there. The term often used for these children is 'school drop outs'. Oxfam, for example, in a major report arguing the benefits of the universal provision of schooling, states that every year 150 million children worldwide start primary school but drop out before they have completed four years of education (Watkins 1999: 1). Various reasons have been put forward to explain this, some of which are based on 'irrational' or cultural deficit factors such as traditional cultural hostility to Western schooling or gender bias and a reluctance to send girls to school. Poverty has also been identified as a contextual factor with the implication that if parents simply had a little more money they would immediately send their children to school in much greater numbers. However, resistance among parents in developing countries may be far more rational and informed than these reasons suggest and the problem may be more with the school than with the family.

'Human capital theory', perhaps the dominant discourse in global debates on education and development, is the idea that education is a form of social and personal investment and that 'rates of return' can be calculated for both society and the individual. The World Bank, for example, has stated that it 'has no genuine rival of equal breadth and rigour' and is used by them to explain the economic success of East Asia (Samoff 1999: 68). However, in many developing countries it may be that the direct costs of sending a child to school (books, uniform, etc.) plus the opportunity costs of labour lost to the family simply outweigh the benefits of schooling. Schooling therefore becomes a bad personal investment. The academic literature on access to education in developing countries recognises that the poor quality of schooling is a disincentive to enrolling pupils at school (Colclough with Lewin 1993) and this is supported by a study of the Dagomba people of northern Ghana which found that school drop out was not just caused by the need for children to work on the farms but because parents knew that the quality of schooling on offer was very poor and in particular because of high levels of teacher absenteeism. Elders in the community put it that 'If the child is not learning in the school and not learning on the farm, where will the child be left?' (Casely-Hayford 1999: 160). Evidence from Pakistan (Farah and Bacchus 1999: 233) equally suggests that parental willingness to send children to school depends more on the availability of good quality schooling than on cultural resistance.

In China, Cheng Kai-Ming (1997) describes a report on low school attendance of girls among the Miao ethnic group. The report identified a number of reasons for low enrolment: economic underdevelopment, parents' discrimination against girls, early marriage, high private costs for parents and the irrelevance and low quality of schooling. Recommendations to overcome low enrolment were reduction of private costs, expansion of the public schools sector, development of vocational education and propaganda and education to discourage early marriage. This study described the key role played by embroidery in the lives of girls in the Miao ethnic group. Embroidery skills were an important indicator of social prestige and were crucial in terms of finding a good husband. In this context embroidery has much higher economic value than schooling. Local educational planners saw low enrolment of girls as 'discrimination against girls' and 'backward institutions' and the solutions lay in 'educating parents' and 'promoting the Marital Law'. Kai-Ming notes that,

> The planners were thus thinking in the framework of universalising basic education and hence anything that presented obstacles to such a course needed to be rectified and changed . . . (but) . . . To the Miao parents and the Miao girls, schooling is something imposed on them because of an importance that is not felt within the community. Meanwhile in order to attend schools, they have to put aside their embroidery exercises, and because of that they worry about their future. Schooling causes problems for girls with immediate effect. From a local perspective, it is therefore not embroidery that is causing the problems but compulsory education that is disturbing their normal lifestyle and culture.
>
> (1997: 78)

However, it is not just a case of poor physical teaching resources and costs – the irrelevant, alienating and even threatening nature of schooling can play a significant part in low enrolment and school drop out. As Samoff notes in relation to the World Bank and human capital theory,

Much of the concern with education as an investment self-consciously ignores the process of education. Adopting an economic systems approach, it focuses on inputs and outputs, leaving inside the black box most of what those involved in education do every day.

(Samoff 1999: 68)

Yet there is considerable evidence that the nature of education offered is a major factor in school drop outs and low enrolment. A DfID/Save the Children study of schooling in India, Mali, Palestinian camps in Lebanon, Liberia, Mozambique, Pakistan, Mongolia, Ethiopia and Peru stated that while many people put their faith in schools to offer children a better chance in life, for some,

the local schools are of such poor quality that it is developmentally healthier for children not to be in them. The school systems are run by inflexible bureaucracies – if children face difficulties in attending because of the constraints of their lives, that is their problem, not one for the school system to sort out. What is taught in school is often incomprehensible (in a language children have never heard) and un-related to their lives. Teachers are harsh, unmotivated and unmotivating. Children drop out, having learnt little.

(Molteno *et al.* 2000: 2)

In India, a recent study concluded that for many parents and children the combination of expense, large classes, unmotivated and absent teachers, an overburdened and meaningless curriculum and an oppressive pedagogy are deeply alienating and account for many of the difficulties of enrolment and retention. It is not so much a problem then of school drop outs, the term often used in the literature on education and development, as school 'push outs' (Alexander 2000: 99). In Mali the DfID/Save the Children study suggested that not only could parents not manage without their children's contribution to the household but that in the minds of the parents work had considerable educational value. It was seen as a process of socialisation, progressively initiating children into work and transmitting skills that would enable them to support themselves and their parents and contribute to the community. Children also accepted the necessity and value of work and there were few instances of oppressive work conditions or abusive punishments. The study noted that,

Two thirds said they liked their work 'a lot' and only a negligible per-centage said 'not at all'. Perhaps this is because children learn by doing tasks with obvious utility, for which they win approval . . . They can move around and be active, they are taught by familiar people, using a language they understand and are given considerable responsibility.

(Molteno *et al.* 2000: 70)

On the other hand the study found that schools were inflexibly organised so that working needs could not be accommodated, had dilapidated buildings, few teaching materials and teachers who 'taught by rote, with no liveliness or active participation. The teachers' style is typically harsh; children are visibly nervous'. As a consequence 'It does not take children or parents long to decide that staying in school will serve no useful purpose' (Molteno *et al.* 2000: 71).

In South America half of those that start school drop out before finishing primary school. The nature of schooling itself plays a large part in this,

> When the teacher is in the classroom, so-called 'frontal teaching' is the norm – four out of five Chilean teachers merely dictate classes to their students, who sit passively in rows. This is what Paulo Freire condemned as the 'banking concept' of education, where teachers see children as empty receptacles in which they must deposit information. Creativity, children's own experiences and knowledge and the ability to work in groups receive short shrift. Children who have never attended school are expected adjust to hours of inactivity, sitting silent and motionless in pain of punishment. Frontal teaching is unable to cope with pupils who miss periods of time due to work commitments, for example, during harvest time. Teachers are unable to deal separately with such children, helping them make up lost ground when they return to class. Not surprisingly, frontal teaching is seen as one of the chief causes of Latin America and the Caribbean's record drop-out and repetition rates.
>
> (Green 1998: 154–155)

One Palestinian writer questions the overall assumption in writing on education and development that education = schooling and that schooling is necessarily good for development,

> A third form of subtle control that development plans often use is a limiting of the options and alternatives in people's minds. Schools, for example, severely limit our imagination and sense of possibilities in the field of education and learning. In most societies today (especially in Third World countries), schools almost certainly monopolise the resources allocated to education and learning. Building learning centres for teachers (and other adults), experimenting with innovative ideas and projects, building communication networks among people, establishing facilities that increase people's access to relevant information (such as libraries), all belong to the broad area of education and learning, and yet they hardly receive any attention or resources (or even recognition). Moreover, many, under the drug of schooling, have forgotten that conversation, walking, reading, writing, playing, and doing, form some of the most wonderful ways of learning. Most of us cannot think of an

alternative to the extremely wasteful, rigid, and ineffective education system that takes up a decade or so of a young person's life.

(Fasheh 1999: 86)

Resistance to formal education in western industrialised nations

At one highly successful London grammar school the mother of a 13 year old met her daughter's religious education teacher at a parents' evening. His first plaintive remark was 'I wish you could tell your daughter to stop asking questions. It's all very well being intellectually curious, but I've got the national curriculum to get through'. Welcome to modern education.

(Russell 2003)

If formal schooling is so good for individuals and has played a key part in Western levels of development, why is there still resistance to it among the consumers? In Western industrialised countries, where primary and secondary education is universally provided for all, there is also considerable disaffection in relation to schooling in some countries,

Disaffection in schools is endemic in American and British society. You'll find it wherever there are institutions called schools and children who are required by law to attend them. It is expressed and defined as persistent truancy, disruptive behaviour, alienation and withdrawal or any combination of these.

(Klein 1999: xii)

In relation to truancy, in England and Wales about a million children every year – 37 per cent of boys and 28 per cent of girls – deliberately miss school for at least half a day. The average for primary school children is five days and for secondary ten days (Klein 1999: 16). The reasons vary from not wanting to go to particular lessons, to avoid particular teachers or tests, to the fear of being bullied, to having to look after siblings at the demand of parents. However 'Many say that school is boring or irrelevant' (Klein 1999: 17). In France government research disclosed that two-thirds of 11–15-year-olds were bored in class and 85 per cent of young teachers have encountered boredom amongst their pupils. The French Minister of Education said that in his own school days '80 per cent of us were as bored as dead rats' but that school was not supposed to be fun and pupils must not confuse it with entertainment. Delegates to a conference on the subject in Paris agreed that bored pupils were likely to be insolent, disruptive and, in extreme cases, violent or drop out of school (Marshall 2003). A survey of OECD countries found that 67 per cent of pupils reported being bored at school in Germany and 66 per cent in both Greece and Spain (cited in UNESCO 2003: 5). In a survey of 15,000 British pupils carried out by the

Guardian newspaper in 2001 some key findings were that the pupils felt that schools were not happy places, that pupils views weren't listened to, that they weren't treated and respected as individuals and that schools were rigid and inflexible institutions (Birkett 2001). In short, though pupils felt that schools weren't necessarily doing them any harm, they weren't necessarily doing them much good either. In one school which has introduced electronic swipe cards to deal with truancy one teacher simply and tellingly commented that despite all the efforts put into reducing truancy, 'Its got to be a school that the kids want to come to. Nobody ever mentions that' (Revell 2002). A letter in the *Guardian* newspaper responded to government criticism of parents condoning truancy in the following way,

> Considering that most parents see school, if they are honest, as a place where they can gratefully dump the kids for free, I think it should be seen as marvellous if a parent wishes to have its small child's company on a shopping trip. And considering how much time is spent in primary schools queuing for your turn to read, being pushed over in the playground, made to line up to go in, queuing again for your milk and then to use the toilet, I am sure that a child would have more personal attention – and more education – during a day off with a parent than anything that can be given to it in school.
>
> (*Guardian* 25/5/2002)

It is also interesting to note that that children labelled as 'school phobic' tend to be of 'average or above average intelligence, with a good social conscience. They can't be controlled by reward and punishment, so promising them a new game for the PlayStation 2 if they go to school for a week won't have any effect' (Moore 2002). Perhaps children who are school phobic have just understood better. In Japan according to a survey conducted by the Ministry of Education, the number of children who were absent for more than 30 days in one year due to 'disliking school' amounted to 20,000 students at the elementary school level (0.26 per cent of the total) and 84,000 at the junior high level (1.87 per cent). Seventy per cent of Japanese public high schools faced this problem in 1998. The actual number of such students is estimated to be four or five times the number provided in official statistics. The physical symptoms of these children include such illnesses as headaches, stomach aches, vomiting and convulsions immediately before they leave for school (Kawaguchi 2000: 502).

Within schooling there can be much day to day resistance and this can take the form of pupil violence against teachers, a phenomenon, if the press is anything to go by, causing increasing official concern in countries such as France, America, Sweden and England. Commenting on this Esteve (2000) cited a UNESCO report from as long ago as 1980 which found that compulsory schooling brought with it an increased risk of violence both against inanimate objects (vandalism) and against fellow pupils and teachers in a situation where young people are forced to continue studying against their will, where they don't see it as doing them any good and where the ensuing boredom and frustration is manifested in violence against the representatives of the institution in which they see themselves confined. What is more is that this can reproduce itself down the generations. An article on aggressive parents who attack teachers noted that, '. . . parents who have no positive memories of school might still regard education as neither a force for change nor for good, but rather as an imposition from an official world. Teachers are their daily contact with that world . . .' (*Times Educational Supplement*, Friday 2/5/2002).

Finally, 'truancy' takes place in a more systematic, planned and organised way in industrialised countries through home-based education, which is an alternative form of provision based on a rejection of both state and private forms of schooling. In 1997 it was estimated that 25,000 families or 50,000 plus children were being educated at home in the UK – approaching 1 per cent of the school population (Meighan 1997: 3). In America figures for the 1997–8 school year were 1.5 million and there had been an annual growth of 15 per cent since 1990 (Apple 2001: 172). Meighan (1997: 2) argued that by the beginning of the twenty-first century it was possible that as much as 10 per cent of the American school-age population could be experiencing home-based education, either on a full-time or flexi-time basis. The reasons that parents and children opt for home education are many and varied. Some do so because they see schooling in a negative way as an authoritarian, indoctrinatory and controlling experience for children, a point that will be more fully developed in a later chapter. This is the main thrust taken by advocates of home schooling such as Meighan (1992) in the UK and Holt (1982) in America. Paradoxically, another strong force behind home-education in America, the religious right, is critical of state schooling because it is not authoritarian and indoctrinatory enough (Apple 2001: Ch. 6).

What is education for?

> Education is a weapon, whose effects depend on who holds it in his hand and at whom it is aimed.
>
> (Joseph Stalin, quoted in Meighan, 1994: 4)

A significant criticism that can be made of the voluminous and highly influential literature on school effectiveness and school improvement is that it does not deal sufficiently with the issue of the diverse goals and purposes of schooling, let alone other forms of education (Harber and Davies 1997). In too much of this literature a false consensus is presented that we all agree on the basic goals of education and that these are reflected in measurable indicators such better examination results, lower truancy rates, more attendance and less drop out. All subsequent discussion becomes a technical matter of how best to achieve these established and agreed upon goals. Rarely is there any discussion about whether the goals themselves are effective. Rarely are questions asked about the fundamental purposes of education – what sort of individuals and what sort of societies are we trying to create? How is education being used to achieve these purposes?

All educational practices have to be understood and only have meaning within their ultimate philosophical and ideological frameworks. Even generally agreed on educational objectives such literacy and numeracy are not fundamental goals as it has to be asked, literacy for what? Numeracy for what? How do we want people to use these skills? Phrases like 'more flexibility', 'more creativity', 'more imagination', 'more independence' or 'more sense of enquiry', are meaningless unless given an ideological context. Even happiness, a commodity in short supply in many formal education systems, is not context free. Let us take the theoretical example of a terrorist training camp. You could have a terrorist training regime which aimed to produce flexible, creative, imaginative and independent terrorists and did so. They may well also be very literate and numerate. And on top of that they may be happy and enjoy their training. Within its own goals it would have to be regarded as effective. But are the *goals themselves* effective? Are terrorists and terror a good thing to produce?

Unfortunately, this is not a purely theoretical or philosophical discussion. Ignoring or playing down the issue of the goals of education can be very dangerous as education systems have been consciously designed and used for purposes of violent evil, have actively participated in the reproduction of violence or, through the sin of omission, have not attempted to educate people to resist violent 'solutions' to social divisions. What it means to be 'educated' therefore is a matter of opinion, not fact. There was a television programme on in January 2002 which was called 'Conspiracy'. The TV guide to the programme started the description of the programme in the following way: 'A dramatisation of the meeting that took place in Berlin on January 20th 1942 in which a roomful of *well-educated lawyers* sat down to a lavish dinner, with brandy and cigars, and voted to gas the entire Jewish population of the western hemisphere'. Hence the importance of the following letter which was sent by an American High School Principal to his teachers at the beginning of every academic year. It concerns education under the Nazis in Germany:

> Dear Teacher, I am the survivor of a concentration camp. My eyes saw what no man should witness. Gas chambers built by learned engineers, children poisoned by educated physicians, infants killed by trained nurses, women and babies shot and burned by high school graduates. So I am suspicious of education. My request is, help your children become more human. Your efforts must never produce learned monsters,

skilled psychopaths, educated Eichmanns. Reading, writing and arithmetic are important only if they serve to make our children more human.

(cited in Pring 1984: Introduction)

The last sentence in particular captures the point being made here. Two British A level students who visited Auschwitz wrote to a newspaper that 'We are so embroiled in education for education's sake that we forget to teach children compassion, respect and how to live without prejudice' (*Guardian* 27/1/2003). In the religious violence that flared up in India in March 2002 a crowd of 10,000 Hindus dragged a Muslim MP, his brother-in-law, his brother-in-law's wife and their two small sons into the street from their house and set them alight. The Police Commissioner for the city where it happened stated 'I hang my head in shame. The people responsible for all this come from the better sections of society. They are not criminals. *Many of them are educated . . .*' (Harding 2002). What was it about their education, or what was missing from their education, that still allowed them to behave in this way? A similar question could be asked in France where the neo-Nazi, racist Groupe Union Defence, responsible for violent attacks on students and others, until recently had its headquarters at the law faculty of the University of Paris. This group has links with Jean-Marie Le Pen, two of whose closest advisers are law professors, one at the University of Paris (*Guardian* 20/7/2002 and 25/4/2002). In South Africa right up to the end of the 1980s highly 'educated', or perhaps more accurately 'qualified', medical doctors were involved in cases of torture under the apartheid regime. Submissions to the Truth and Reconciliation Commission contradicted the notion that doctors who colluded with security forces in human rights abuses were just 'a few bad apples' but that abuses arose in a context in which the entire fabric of the health service was permeated by apartheid (*Mercury*, Durban 17/6/97). As was the education system that supplied the health service under apartheid.

In the Rwandan genocide of 1994 when between 800,000 and a million people (one-eighth of its population) were murdered in the space of a few weeks, teachers from a Hutu ethnic background commonly denounced their Tutsi pupils to the militia or even directly killed them themselves. Indeed, the role of schooling in this genocide poses some very serious and important questions about why and how we educate in all societies. As two commentators on the Rwandan genocide put it,

> The role of well-educated persons in the conception, planning and execution of the genocide requires explanation; any attempt at explanation must consider how it was possible that their education did not render genocide unthinkable. The active involvement of children and young people in carrying out the violence, sometimes against their

teachers and fellow pupils, raises further questions about the *kind* of education they received.

(Retamal and Aedo-Richmond 1998: 16)

It would be interesting to survey the educational qualifications of the world's tyrants and dictators of the twentieth and now early twenty-first century to see the levels of qualification they obtained.

The above examples illustrate that education can be used to promote violence, that education doesn't necessarily prevent the use of violence and that education can be used in the pursuit of very negative and undesirable goals. However, it is not always so clear-cut or straightforward. In the liberation struggles in Africa in the 1970s and 1980s (for example, Zimbabwe, Namibia and South Africa) liberation movements had to organise along 'terrorist' lines in order to overcome undemocratic, oppressive and violent regimes. Training and education were very much part of their organisational structure (Harber 1989, 1997a). A study of the backgrounds of dead Hizbullah militants and Palestinian suicide bombers by the National Bureau of Economic Research in America found that they came predominantly from the more educated sections of the population (cited in Walker 2002). The key question is whether the means justify the end – are the political goals and the education used to achieve them just and justifiable? This raises the issue of what the fundamental goals of education should be. For this writer they are concerned with democracy and peace and are discussed in the last chapter of this book. The question that has to be asked is 'is the use of violence, and the education and training that supports it, unavoidable and essential for the eventual creation of a more democratic and peaceful society?' Answers to this question are also seldom straightforward. In Zimbabwe at the time of writing, the oppressive regime of Robert Mugabe does not provide a particularly good justification for the violence of the liberation war of the 1970s. However, it could equally well be argued that this was the only way to remove the undemocratic colonial regime and was therefore a necessary means to an end even if the end is proving difficult and painful to achieve.

Conclusion

Formal education and schooling isn't automatically and inevitably of benefit to individuals and societies. Indeed, as the graphic and violent examples used here demonstrate, everything depends on the nature, purposes and priorities of education, the definition of what it means to be educated and resulting educational practices. What is missing in education is often as important as what is taught. Many more examples of schooling's role as an agent of violence will be described in the book in the chapters discussing the different ways in which schools are complicit in violence. However, before we explore the ways in which schools can act as violent and harmful institutions it is necessary to explore what it is about schooling that makes its violent role possible. What are the key aspects of schooling that create an organisational environment that can be supportive of violence? The next chapter analyses the organisationally dominant model of schooling internationally – authoritarianism.

2 Authoritarian schooling

State Parties shall assure to the child who is capable of forming his or her own views the right to express those views freely in all matters affecting the child, the views of the child being given due weight in accordance with the age and maturity of the child.

(Article 12, UN Convention on the Rights of the Child,
signed by every country in the world except America and Somalia)

Students do not participate in choosing the goals, the curriculum or the manner of working. These things are chosen for the students. Students have no part in the choice of teaching personnel, nor any voice in educational policy. Likewise the teachers often have no voice in choosing their administrative officers . . . All this is in striking contrast to all the teaching about the virtues of democracy, the importance of the 'free world' and the like. The political practices of the school stand in most striking contrast to what is taught. While being taught that freedom and responsibility are the glorious features of our democracy, students are experiencing powerlessness and having almost no opportunity to exercise choice or carry responsibility.

(Carl Rogers quoted in *Education Now* 2002)

Introduction

Later in this book a range of ways in which schooling is experienced as a violent institution by students will be discussed and unpleasant and disturbing examples will be used to support the argument. It is my contention that this negative dimension of schooling has been consistently played down or ignored internationally in governmental policy documents and in the majority of academic writing and research where education in the form of schooling is presented and accepted too readily as a given good. This chapter is concerned with what it is about schooling that lends itself to either actively participating in violence or passively acquiescing in the reproduction of violence in the wider society. It is argued that, despite most countries having signed the UN Convention on the Rights of the Child, for the majority of pupils schooling is an essentially authoritarian experience and that this has important implications for the later discussions of modes of schooling and violence. This is because authoritarian organisation provides an environment where pupils' rights, needs and feelings can too readily be ignored or suppressed and where it is difficult for teachers or pupils to act independently and to critique and challenge dominant social and political orthodoxies, including those that lead to violent behaviour and conflict. Authoritarian schools are therefore schools that reproduce and perpetrate not only the socio-economic and political inequalities of the surrounding society but also the violent relationships that often go with them. Moreover, as we began to see in Chapter 1, rejection by pupils of imposed authoritarian forms can itself lead to violence. This chapter discusses the nature and prevalence of authoritarian forms of schooling, while Chapter 3 discusses different types of school violence and their relationship to authoritarianism and Chapter 4 discusses historical and sociological explanations for authoritarianism as the dominant mode of school organisation.

It is important here to add a note about a tension between universalism and contextuality in understanding the role of schooling as an agency of violence. At the heart of much post-modern writing is a rejection of universal theories and generalised 'iron laws' of society and development in favour of an emphasis on the particularities and diversity of different specific contexts (Usher and Edwards 1994; Meighan and Siraj-Blatchford 1997). Indeed, the present writer has argued for the need to understand the specific contexts of developing countries in relation to the generalised statements of literature stemming from Western, industrialised nations about school effectiveness and school management (Harber and Davies 1997). However, this book emphasises both the universal and the particular. As is argued in this chapter and Chapter 3, authoritarianism or 'repressive violence' forms a very common, dominant form of school and classroom organisation internationally and this will be explained in terms of the historical origins of mass formal schooling and its subsequent geographical spread in Chapter 4. Moreover, the final chapter of this book argues for a global emphasis on education for democracy and peace. While not 'iron laws' in the sense of, for example, Marxism or modernisation theory, these are internationally generalised arguments of analysis, explanation and, in the case of democracy and peace, prescription. On the other hand, while schooling is rarely completely free from violence anywhere, it is hoped that a sufficiently wide range of examples from different contexts is provided to suggest that the specific ways in which schooling plays itself out in terms of different types, manifestations and levels of violence varies from one cultural, economic and political context to another.

Schooling and compulsion

Before examining the nature and widespread occurrence of authoritarian school and classroom organisation one important feature of schooling in many countries ought to be noted. This is the element of compulsion involved. In many Western countries education is compulsory until the end of secondary level and this is often interpreted (sometimes incorrectly) as meaning schooling. In many developing countries governments would make schooling compulsory if the resources were there to provide it for all. A number of writers, however, see the attempt to make schooling compulsory as an act of violence in itself. Meighan, for example, argues that it is a massive indictment that children do not go to school by choice but by compulsion, which is an abuse of human rights,

> The problem with most discussions about education is that the essential coercive and indoctrinational cultures of mass schooling are overlooked. In blunt terms, based on the current model of the compulsory day-detention centre, the school itself is a bully institution. When you take the free will out of education, that turns it into schooling.
>
> (1999: 4)

Yet many children for much of the time don't want to be in school in the first place. John Cosgrove, a deputy headteacher with over twenty years' experience in English primary and secondary schools, has also commented on the forced nature of some schooling systems and the connection with authoritarian power relationships inside schools,

> Let's not kid ourselves. Even in the easiest, best motivated schools, many of the pupils, much of the time, would rather not be there. Children do not choose to go to school. The choice is made for them. Once in school, more or less unwillingly, pupils are presented with activities chosen for them and they are given no option about attempting them. There do exist schools where pupils have a free choice about which lessons to attend, and whether or not they complete assignments, but such institutions are as rare as primroses flowering on an English New Year's Day . . . For the most part schools make children do things.
>
> (Cosgrove 2000: 51)

As we saw in Chapter 1, schooling is not necessarily universally or automatically perceived as beneficial and throughout this book further reasons why this might be the case will be explored. Indeed, if the benefits of schooling were so patently obvious, the extent to which schools and other agencies go to get pupils into them would not be quite so extraordinary. On the inducement side, one school in Halifax, UK is offering pupils cash rewards for good attendance. Pupils who do not miss a single day in a year can earn up to £80.00 (*Times Educational Supplement* 30/11/2001). Children who attend a primary school in Newcastle, UK will be rewarded with a free meal at a local restaurant (*Times Educational Supplement* 3/5/2002). There is nothing new about this in the UK as this comment on the introduction of compulsory mass schooling at the end of the nineteenth century makes clear,

> In the years after 1870, rewards were offered by schools to encourage attendance, among which were certificates of merit and the return of fees. These inducements had a beneficial influence on the attendance at school of numbers of children, but not on persistent truants in the interest of whom education had been made obligatory.
>
> (Ellis 1985: 34)

On the other hand, those who do 'truant' (originally a word for a medieval French bandit) are being tracked in ever more sophisticated ways. In Singapore and the UK mobile phones and text messages are being used to contact parents when a child is absent without notification (*Times Educational Supplement* 13/4/2001; *Guardian* 1/6/2001). In Germany an electronics company has developed a tracker which can be sown into a school uniform or school bag which will use global positioning satellite technology and be able to pinpoint a truanting child to within five metres and alert teachers and parents (Leidig 2000). In the UK parents have been fined and sent to jail because their children have played truant. Perhaps if schools were more inviting places then truancy, under-enrolment and push outs would not be such problematic issues.

Authoritarianism and learning

Authoritarianism is a type of political system where the government is not representative of the people and where the final power to remove a government is not in the hands of the voters as there are no genuinely free and fair elections. There is no free political choice and the government is not accountable to the people for its actions. As the government is not accountable it is free to do as it wishes and there are therefore no guaranteed human rights. Citizens have little say in how the country is run and rule is by edict and dictat. Single party and military regimes fall into this category. The political culture associated with such regimes is not characterised by full information, regular discussion and encouragement of a range of viewpoints. Diversity, critical thought and participation are not encouraged or are suppressed. The leaders know they have the right answers and the role of the people is to obey and do what they are told. Those who do not obey are punished accordingly. Communication is top-down and hierarchical. The ideal citizen is one who is submissive, behaves according to the wishes of the regime, respects authority and doesn't ask questions. In its most extreme form it has been described as totalitarian as the state attempts closely and directly to control all aspects of life, including the economy, the media, religion, schooling and family life as well as government policy and political activity. Nazi Germany, the Soviet Union and Communist

China, particularly under Mao Tse-tung, are examples of states that have been described as totalitarian. State sponsored violence exercised by the police, secret police and army is a feature of both authoritarian and totalitarian regimes where it is used to suppress criticism and opposition and punish those responsible.

An important feature of authoritarianism and totalitarianism is the use of indoctrination to control the population and maintain compliance and obedience. In a situation where there is a single group that has a monopoly of power they are in a position to try to use the media and the education system to reinforce their ideology. Indoctrination is the intentional inculcation of values and beliefs as truths. The process may involve deliberately falsifying or ignoring evidence, presenting it in a biased way and denigrating alternatives. Less extreme than indoctrination but more common, and probably more effective, is what can be termed socialisation. This is where certain values and attitudes are given preference and taken more seriously, even though other viewpoints and opinions may be available and openly expressed by some in the wider society. This is what the Italian writer Antonio Gramsci (1977) described as 'hegemonic' ideas, that is the dominant ideas in a society that support the ruling group and which are given far greater credence than other ideas in the media and in the education system. Examples might include dominant religious values, nationalism and patriotism, the identification of a particular enemy, competition, individualism, monarchy, meritocracy and patriarchy. Authoritarianism itself is one such set of political values. The aim is to create predispositions to certain values and beliefs in the minds of learners so that they are given more weight than others and indeed become taken as granted and seen as natural and inevitable. Schooling is an important agent of political socialisation and there are a number of academic studies of the role of schooling in political socialisation internationally (see, for example, Dawson *et al.* 1977; Stacey 1978; Harber 1989; Harber 1991; Ichilov 1990; Apple 2001; Bray and Lee 2001).

The opposite to these authoritarian forms of learning is genuine education where there is an attempt to create critical awareness, ideas and values by open, balanced discussion and analysis of a range of evidence and opinions, including non-dominant ones. This has an underlying democratic ideology of personal freedom and informed political choice. This is not associated with authoritarian or totalitarian forms of government and, as will be argued below, is still insufficiently associated with schooling even in those countries with democratically elected governments. A comparative discussion of the tensions between political socialisation and political education in the South African and English education systems which covers a wide range of themes, including various forms of violence in relation to race, gender, punishment and sexuality, is provided in Carter and colleagues (2003).

Schooling and authoritarianism

There have been those from Aristotle onwards who have seen a connection between child-rearing practices and different types of political regime,

> the emphasis upon obedience training, the use of severe physical punishment, and a hierarchically arranged inter-personal environment seem to be correlated with an authoritarian political system, while emphasis upon training in sharing and co-operative effort, the use of non-physical discipline, and a free-group environment with no pro-nounced status distinctions seems to be correlated with an egalitarian political system.
>
> (Levine 1963: 296)

In the same way that political systems can be totalitarian, authoritarian or democratic so can the institutions of child-rearing, including formal educa-tion. In terms of schooling, the dominant or hegemonic model globally, with exceptions that will be discussed later in the book, is authoritarian rather than democratic. Education for and in democracy, human rights and critical awareness is not a primary characteristic of the majority of schooling. While the degree of harshness and despotism within authoritar-ian schools varies from context to context and from institution to institu-tion, in the majority of schools power over what is taught and learned, how it is taught and learned, where it is taught and learned, when it is taught and learned and what the general learning environment is like is not in the hands of pupils. It is predominantly government officials, head-teachers and teachers who decide, not learners. Most schools are essentially authoritarian institutions, however benevolent or benign that authori-tarianism is and whatever beneficial aspects of learning are imparted. In this authoritarian situation of relative powerlessness and neglect of their human rights pupils can be mistreated violently or be influenced by poten-tially violent beliefs because the dominant norms and behaviours of the wider society are shared, not challenged, by many adults in the formal education system. Later chapters will explore violent physical punishment, sexual violence, stress and anxiety, racial violence and militarisation as ways in which schools can and do act violently towards pupils. The rest of this chapter reviews international evidence on the predominantly authori-tarian nature of schooling and violent reaction to it.

The following sections briefly survey literature which comments on power relationships between teachers and taught internationally. The evi-dence reviewed here, given the vast global literature on education, has had to be selective, though an attempt has been made to refer to most geo-graphical regions. Nevertheless, the evidence does indeed suggest that authoritarian relationships are a dominant theme of schooling internation-ally and, while there are always exceptions, authoritarian relationships are a more common characteristic of most schooling systems than democratic relationships.

However, before reviewing this literature, a brief note on the role of the headteacher is relevant. Research that compared 200 headteachers in Britain with 200 senior managers and directors of multinational companies found that heads were prone to an authoritarian style, issuing orders and expecting obedience (Kelly 2000). This reinforces earlier evidence and analysis of the micro-political role of the headteacher (Harber 1992: Ch. 2; Davies 1994: Ch. 2). In their book on school effectiveness Holmes and Wynne (1989: 58) describe the most frequently found type of headteacher as the 'benevolent despot', a term that was used to describe and analyse the role of headteachers in developing countries (Harber and Davies 1997: Ch. 4). If the leader at the apex of school organisation can often be described as a despot, benevolent or otherwise, because of lack of, or only nominal, levels of staff and pupil participation in decision making, then it shouldn't be too surprising if school and classroom organisation reflect this.

Africa

In Africa schools have been characterised by hierarchical organisation, rote learning and teacher-centred classrooms,

> Throughout Africa . . . lessons involve frequent oral recitation of vocabulary or arithmetic exercises, delivered in unison by all pupils. This mechanical process, set by the curricula or teacher guide, helps control and engage the fifty to ninety restless pupils that commonly sit before the teacher. Thus curricular content helps signal and legitimate certain forms of authority and human interaction which come to be seen as normal in a modern (hierarchical) organisation.
>
> (Fuller 1991: 68)

Fuller uses evidence from Malawi (and recent visits to schools in Malawi by the writer suggest that little has changed in this respect). Similar evidence of teacher domination of lessons and rote learning and of the generally authoritarian nature of schools and classrooms exists in relation, for example, to Botswana (Prophet and Rowell 1990; Tabulawa 1995; Tafa 2002), Ghana (Hedges 2002), Nigeria (Harber 1989), Zimbabwe (Nagel 1992; Davies 1993; Bourne *et al.* 1998) and Zambia (Serpell 1993). In Mozambique one study ranked different pupil activities by the amount of time pupils spend on them. Ranked first was listening to teachers – the probability is that a pupil will get to speak once every second day and even then will be repeating the teacher's sentences or sentences from the textbook. Second in importance is waiting – for the teacher to begin the lesson, for the teacher to write things on the board, for their classmates to finish exercises which they have already finished and for their work to be corrected. The third most common activity was copying. The author comments that 'The dominant classroom interaction pattern, then, seems to be that of overwhelmingly passive pupils whose activities are limited to be almost entirely reproductive in nature' (Palme 1997: 196). In South Africa the rigidly authoritarian system of schooling was replaced by an education policy based on principles of democracy and human rights in 1994 but this is inevitably proving difficult and slow to implement (Harber 2001a). Even in the then socialist Tanzania, and despite the aims of education for self-reliance, not only was caning common but one very common teaching method was 'copy-copy' where the teacher copies notes or words from a textbook or notebook onto the blackboard. The students then copy these into their own notebooks and 'copy' their notes onto paper from memorisation in the examinations (Mbilinyi 1979). Such authoritarian relationships also often involve the use of violence in the form of corporal punishment and this is discussed further in Chapter 4.

Asia

In Chinese countries, 'The teacher as high authority figure seems pan-Chinese, a fact verified by the dominance of the lecture method and teacher-centred classrooms not only in Taiwan but also in the People's Republic and Hong Kong' (Meyer 1988: 22).

In reviewing studies of classrooms in China, Biggs (1996: 56) rightly stresses the subtleties and contextual complexities of teacher–student classroom interaction (as would be necessary anywhere) but nevertheless notes that despite these caveats teachers and schools still have to be described as authoritarian because there is still only one 'right way'. He also notes that such benevolent authoritarianism is also the approach favoured by many Westerners in the classroom, a point that will be discussed below. Similar teacher-centred lecturing methods are also predominant in Thailand, Nepal and the Philippines (Lockheed 1993: 31–32). In a recent study of the practice of civic education in Hong Kong, Taiwan, Japan and Thailand (as well as America and Australia) one general conclusion was,

> from the perspective of pupils, there was often a very clear awareness of the disjuncture between their school's precepts and its practices. It was the latter that were seen to define the values that the school thought were important. The pupils were acutely aware when the rhetoric of school policy was seen to be in conflict with other messages that were conveyed, especially with regard to the high value placed on obedience and on passing high stake examinations. These values were most powerfully manifested not in the formal curriculum but through the organisation of school activities and the various elements that comprise the hidden or implicit curriculum.
>
> (Morris and Cogan 2001: 119)

In Japan: 'It is well known that comparatively strict rules have governed the classroom until recently . . . This has resulted from rules stipulated by the school and the strict disciplinary measures consequent upon violation of such rules, which sometimes include corporal punishment' (Kawaguchi 2000: 500). Hanuki (2000) also describes a schooling system in Japan which is oppressive and based on 'severe control' of children, where corporal punishment is still used, where there is excessive pressure from competitive examinations and where children's freedom of expression is severely limited. As a result many children are not happy at school and there is considerable student resistance and rebellion. Sullivan (1996) also comments on the authoritarian order and harsh discipline in Japanese schools where students can be punished for the most minor breaches of dress code. Thousands of schoolgirls buy 'sock glue' to keep their white ankle socks at a uniform height, feeling the pressure to be exactly like everyone else. The mayor of one city in Japan insisted that teachers also wear uniforms. In South Korea, Kang (2002) describes a situation where, though there has been some progress towards democracy and human rights in education since the installation of a civilian government in 1998, there is still much resistance in schools. Schools still tend to be highly competitive, standardised, inflexible and uniform. Students have little say in what is taught and how or how the school is run.

In Thailand schooling rote learning has traditionally been the norm and questioning the teacher has been perceived as rude and challenging. The 1999 Education Act tried to reform schooling to make it child-centred but there are large problems in trying to implement the reforms. According to the Director of the Bureau of Teacher Education Development the key problem is changing the mind-set of both the lecturers at the 41 teacher training institutes and the teachers in the 40,000 state school classrooms. The Director commented that 'in their hearts they do not believe in the new way of teaching' and that some saw questions as challenging their authority (East 2001).

A study of schools in Papua New Guinea found that,

> The three major requirements that students must display in order to be considered a 'good' student by the majority of teachers included: (1) that the student is obedient and listens to the teacher, (2) that he or she behaves well in class and (3) that he or she is a quiet person who concentrates well . . . Not one teacher, for example, suggested to me that a good student might sometimes question a teacher's or anyone else's authority.
>
> (Fife 1997: 102–103)

Similarly, a study of school improvement in Indonesia noted that 'Observing lessons showed that teachers still practice whole-class instruction. Students are not encouraged to participate actively' (Van Der Werf *et al.*

2000: 353). Alexander's (2000) detailed study of primary school classroom practice in five countries included India. Here the teacher-centred, transmission model of teaching is overwhelmingly predominant, described as the 'rite of rote'. There was a large gap between teachers' espoused theory (activity method, group work, individual attention and joyful learning) with observed classroom practice. Instruction was 'unremittingly didactic with students sat in rows, taking notes and repeating what they had been told'. Overall, Alexander describes Indian primary education as characterised by 'regimentation and ritualization' (2000: 307, 334, 387).

Europe

While some countries in Europe, such as Germany, Holland, Denmark and Sweden, have made considerable progress towards educating for human rights and democracy (Davies and Kirkpatrick 2000), others retain a strong and even dominant element of authoritarianism in their school organisation and teaching. In terms of Western Europe the need to be selective means that three countries will be described – Britain, France and Portugal. This is because these are three countries with a considerable colonial legacy and historical impact on education globally, an important theme in the next chapter. In terms of Eastern Europe, Russia has been selected as a case study because for five decades until the end of the Cold War it established the model for the then Eastern Bloc's education system and since then has attempted to democratise its education system.

Charles Handy, at the time a Professor of Business organisations, turned his attention to British secondary schools in the 1980s and concluded that the nearest model of organisational style he could come up with in analysing schools was prisons in that the inmates' routine is disrupted every 40 minutes, they change their place of work and supervisors constantly, they have no place to call their own and they are often forbidden to communicate with each other. He also argued that if you look at schools in another way then they are more like factories and the pupils like products which are inspected at the end of the production line, sometimes rejected as substandard and then stamped 'Maths', 'English', 'History', etc. (Handy 1984). Indeed, in a survey of adults ranging in age from under 25 to over 65 carried out in 1998 which asked respondents to reflect on their citizenship skills, a majority said that schooling had either had no effect or a negative effect on their ability to deal with difference and conflict, to voice ideas and opinions, to act independently if you think it is right, to take responsibility and to assume that your voice will be heard and taken into account (Benn 2000).

Since then an already authoritarian situation has been made worse by the introduction of the centralised and prescriptive national curriculum in 1988. Alexander's five nation comparative study described it as the 'most centralised and ruthlessly policed' (2000: 532). Research by MORI, who conduct public attitude surveys, asked pupils in England to name three things they do most often. While other activities such as discussion did feature in the responses, the two most common were copying from a board or a book (58 per cent) and listening to their teacher (39 per cent) (Lucas 2000). A recent study of the actual operation of the national curriculum over a five-year period involving 7000 pupils, 250 teachers and the observation of 97 lessons in primary, secondary and tertiary educational institutions concluded that,

> the national curriculum, in operation, enforced a limited course restricted to the rote-learning of subject-specific knowledge so that pupils may perform well in written tests of memory. It is my contention that this knowledge-based, assessment driven curriculum demands didactic drill-training to ensure examination success; and that such a pedagogy suppresses the development of a critical disposition, so that the school leaver becomes a passive serf or discontented outlaw, rather than an emancipated citizen or productive worker.
>
> (Griffith 2000: xvii)

French classrooms have also been characterised as 'catechistic' and having a didactic, highly authoritarian teaching style with an emphasis more on the product than the process of learning and on there being one right answer (Broadfoot 1999). Alexander's observation of lessons in France concurs with this and he also uses the word 'didactic' and also describes the centrally prescribed curriculum in France as sitting uncomfortably with social and political pluralism and knowledge in French schools as 'received, not negotiated or reflexive'. He thinks it is no coincidence that one of the most sustained criticisms of education as cultural and social reproduction comes from France in the shape of the work of Pierre Bourdieu (Alexander 2000: 62, 420).

Campos (1991) notes that surveys of young people in Portugal have revealed passivity in relation to participation in political life and distrust of the democratic system. While acknowledging that the schooling is not the only factor influencing the situation, he argues that research has underlined the negative role played by the school's hidden curriculum. Methodology in school textbooks does not encourage co-operation, participation and responsibility, observed teaching methods tend to lead to dependency and competition, giving pupils neither a say in decisions nor responsibility for managing projects. He quotes a number of research studies to support this including one study which concluded not only that work in Portuguese classrooms remained essentially teacher-centred but that overpopulation in schools, inadequate material conditions and the lack of explicit rules governing collective life encourage an apprenticeship of irresponsibility, violence, oppression and a struggle for survival far more than they promote responsibility and cooperation.

In the Soviet Union early experimentation in education immediately after the Revolution of 1917 gave way to Communist Party ideological control and authoritarian teaching methods. As Schweisfurth puts it Soviet schools were 'rigidly conformist (by decree and by habit) and highly disciplined, and teaching was based on the delivery of the state curriculum (2002a: 57). Since the collapse of the Soviet Union and single party communist rule in Eastern Europe attempts have been made to democratise education systems as described, for example, by Dneprov (1995). However, Alexander's empirical study of schools and classrooms in Russia strongly suggests that, as elsewhere, old habits die hard and that there is a significant gap between teachers' espousal of democratic rhetoric and their actual teaching methods. He describes contemporary Russian classrooms as rule-bound, regimented, teacher-controlled and didactic with routines verging on the ritualistic. As in India and France teachers worked with curriculum labels and syllabuses laid down for them, often using centrally prescribed textbooks (2000: 78, 386/7, 412, 420, 553). In terms of school management, one study of a project aimed at helping Russian headteachers operate in a more democratic manner found that 70 years of communist rule had reinforced the importance of obedience and discipline making headteachers very reluctant to delegate and teachers reluctant to participate and accept responsibility (Shaw and Ormston 2001).

The Middle East and Arab States

Schools and classrooms in this region do not seem so widely researched and written about as other regions, though the texts that discuss formal schooling in these countries do tend to refer to the authoritarian learning context. Stating that most education systems in Arab states exist in the context of authoritarian political regimes, Massialas and Jarrar comment that, 'the Arab classroom teaches reverence to authority figures and complete submission to their will; it teaches not to question traditional sources of knowledge and wisdom' (1991: 144–145). Similarly Badran comments that,

> Political instability in the Middle East has contributed to governments in the area striving to create a high degree of intellectual conformity among citizenry – this having been judged a prerequisite to stability. But it has also resulted in too much academic sterility. Many of the region's brightest minds have emigrated to countries where they enjoy intellectual freedom and are encouraged to develop their own ideas. The situation cannot be changed easily or quickly, but no government can expect its education system to turn out bright and creative people if it does not encourage an intellectual environment of free enquiry.
>
> (Badran 1989: 316)

Another writer on education in the Middle East argues that there is a need to move away from absolutes and eternal givens to encouraging critical, questioning thinking. This writer links authoritarian education in the Middle East to Paulo Freire, further discussed below,

> To adopt Freire's terminology, education in the Arab world has to become problem posing, not problem solving. The teacher's task must be to present the topic as a problem, the content of which mediates it, and not simply discourse on it, extend it or hand it over, as if it were a matter of something already done, completely finished.
>
> (Meyer 1984: 148–149)

Again, as with other regions this state-controlled form of authoritarian schooling is contested and there are exceptions but, as elsewhere, it does seem to be the dominant model.

North America

The authoritarian nature of schooling in America has been a consistent theme of critics such as John Holt, John Taylor Gatto, Neil Postman and Charles Weingartner, Carl Rogers and Paul Goodman. The following are two examples cited from the list provided at the end of the book:

> It is not possible to spend any prolonged period of time visiting public school classrooms without being appalled by the mutilation visible everywhere – mutilation of spontaneity, of joy in learning, or pleasure in creating, or sense of self . . . Because adults take the schools so much for granted, they fail to appreciate what grim, joyless places most American schools are (they are much the same in most countries), how oppressive and petty are the rules by which they are governed, how intellectually sterile and aesthetically barren the atmosphere, what an appalling lack of civility obtains on the part of teachers and principals, what contempt they unconsciously display for students as students.
>
> (Charles Siberman)

> American kids like watching violence on TV and in the movies because violence is being done to them, both at school and at home. It builds up a tremendous amount of anger . . . The problem is not violence on TV. That's a symptom . . . The real problem is the violence of anti-life, un-affectionate, and punitive homes, and disempowering, deadening compulsory schooling, all presented with an uncomprehending smile.
>
> (Jerry Mintz)

A nation-wide survey in the United States demonstrated that schooling occurs almost entirely in a teacher-directed manner. The author says,

> Somewhere, I suspect down in the elementary school, probably in the fifth and sixth grades, a subtle shift occurs. The curriculum subjects, topics, textbooks, workbooks and the rest – come between the teacher and the student. Young humans come to be viewed only as students, valued primarily for their academic aptitude and industry rather than as individual persons preoccupied with the physical, social and personal needs unique to their personal circumstances and stage in life.
>
> (Goodlad 1984: 80)

The fact that a book on four case studies of democratic public schools in America excited a considerable amount of interest (Apple and Beane 1999: xvii) is encouraging but also highlights how unusual they are and, as the authors themselves demonstrate, how they have been established and survived despite the generally hostile political and educational climate of centralisation, testing, competition, conformity to 'standards', bureaucratic authority and managerialism. Alexander's (2000) research in American primary schools showed them to be more relaxed and caring places that tried to create a sense of community and to stimulate pupil interest but there was little sign in the observational data of pupils having any say in school rules or the content of the curriculum. Moreover, as with teachers in the UK, France, India and Russia, teachers spoke more frequently than their pupils and for longer at a time (Alexander 2000: 428).

In Canada, Fullan and his colleagues used 3600 questionnaires in a survey of students in Ontario schools. They found that,

- only a minority of students think that teachers understand their point of view and the proportion decreases with educational level
- less than one fifth of the students reported that teachers asked for their opinions and ideas in deciding what or how to teach
- principals and vice principals were not seen as listening to or being influenced by students
- substantial percentages of students, including one out of every two high school students, reported that 'most of my classes are boring'.

(Fullan 1991: 171)

South and Central America and the Caribbean

A survey of fourteen countries in South and Central America found that, with the single exception of the Escuela Nueva or New School Programme in Colombia which will be discussed later in the book, although teachers claimed to use a variety of teaching methods such as role play, debate, conferences, lectures, guest speakers and field trips, the students responded by saying that they experienced only listening to the teacher, memorising, writing down and copying (Villegas-Reimers 1993). However, schools in Colombia outside of this Programme have been described as rigid, authoritarian, favouring rote learning and discouraging inquiry, questioning and a critical approach (Abello 1997: 459, 461). A study of schooling and violence in Colombia for UNESCO's International Bureau of Education argued that the function of schools was control, homogenisation and reproduction. Time is controlled by strict timetables where everyone does the same thing at the same time and physical space is used as a means of controlling and watching over all of the activities undertaken at the school. Absolute power is incarnated in the image of the teacher and this fluctuates between the strict application of the rules to the administration of judgements and condemnation of the students' attitudes, behaviours, feelings and abilities at times at the teacher's whim. Students have no say in the curriculum which is taught in a dogmatic and authoritarian manner generating discrimination, school failures and drop out (Bernal 1997: 36–37).

One study of schools in Brazil noted that,

> There was little oral interaction between teacher and students over instructional issues. The dominant type of schoolwork was solitary work in textbooks, workbooks, notebooks and worksheets. Children are required to do fill-in types of exercises that called for short answers to factual questions. This typically followed a short and verbally economical introduction by the teacher of some new topic . . .Verbal interaction between teachers and students was limited to procedural issues, control and to economical question-and-answer sequences. There is little feedback.
>
> (cited in Leonardos 1993: 71)

In Mexico, Martin (1994: 174–175) describes a situation where teachers take a more restricted and instrumental view over what should be controlled, but nevertheless exercise control in an authoritarian manner. In Jamaica, observers noted that 59 per cent of classroom time was taken up by teacher talk, with teachers dominating the lessons and posing few open-ended questions (Jennings-Wray 1984).

Despite the revolution in Cuba the method of instruction has been described as catechistic, an authoritarian teacher-centred approach characterised by a single teacher talking at a class of passive students (Bowles 1976). Likewise Nicaragua under the Sandinistas also failed to break out of this authoritarian, 'one right answer' mould (Green 1998: 156).

One of the most well-known critiques of authoritarian forms of education originated from Brazil. This is Paulo Freire's 'banking education', whereby knowledge (as defined by the teacher) is 'deposited' in the student and on which he or she is later expected to 'capitalise'. It implies a view of knowledge as static, as made and finished and of learners as empty and lacking consciousness. Freire cites ten ways in which this sort of student–teacher relationship manifests itself:

1. The teacher teaches and the students are taught.
2. The teacher knows everything and the students know nothing.
3. The teacher thinks and the students are thought about.
4. The teacher talks and the students listen – meekly.
5. The teacher disciplines and the students are disciplined.
6. The teacher chooses and enforces his or her choice and the students comply.
7. The teacher acts and the students have the illusion of acting through the action of the teacher.
8. The teacher chooses the programme content and the students comply.
9. The teacher confuses the authority of knowledge with professional authority which he or she sets in opposition to the freedom of the students.
10. The teacher is the subject of the learning process while the pupils are mere objects.

(Freire 1972: 46–47)

Critical education, on the other hand, means involving students in their own learning and interpretation of the world through dialogue, questioning, participation and discussion.

Authoritarian élite socialisation

The other side of the authoritarian coin are the expensive private schools which exist internationally and which put the authority in authoritarian through providing an education which emphasises an expectation of leadership. In Britain traditionally these are the famous 'public' schools such as Eton, Harrow and Winchester and in France they are the Lycées. This model, as with mass schooling, was exported internationally through colonialism. In Africa, for example, they have played a significant role in the recruitment of political élites (Harber 1989: 6–9). One particularly notable example is Kamuzu Academy in Malawi which became known as the 'Eton in the bush' and was set up by the then President Hastings Banda deliberately for the purpose of élite recruitment and is now an expensive private school in an otherwise very poor country (Carroll 2002).

An example of how this type of élite schooling works is Michaelhouse School in KwaZulu Natal, South Africa which charges 32,000 rand a year and which is based on the model of the British public school. Michaelhouse operates what it calls the 'cack' system – cacks being the term by which all first years are known, meaning 'scum of the earth'. Like the 'fagging' system in British public schools, junior students are expected to serve and do tasks for senior students. In the past this was enforced with a great deal of physical punishment. Although it does not now involve this element of brutality the practice remains in place (Bauer 1996). The essence of this practice is that the younger students serve an apprenticeship in authority commencing at the bottom of the ladder. The principle which underlies this is subordination as a necessary prerequisite for superordination, i.e. those who expect to give commands (both inside the school and later outside) should have experience of receiving them. Such future expectations of leadership are reinforced by the acknowledged élite status of the school which is manifested in its buildings and traditions and reflected in the post-school professional connections and opportunities it provides.

Violence and authoritarian schooling

The main purpose of this chapter has been to establish the authoritarian nature of much of formal schooling internationally before going on to explain in Chapter 3 why it is like this. Given the predominantly authoritarian nature of a formal schooling, it is not surprising that there is pupil resistance to schooling. Indeed, it is perhaps surprising that there isn't more resistance. But resistance to schooling there is and resistance there always has been – sometimes violent resistance. Although a generally neglected area in the academic study of education, one exception is Robert Adams' book *Protests by Pupils* (1991) in which he documents pupil resistance to schooling in England and in a number of other countries over a very long period of time, including the school strikes of 1911 in England which involved up to a *million* young people. As he says at the beginning of the book 'it will become apparent that protests by pupils should be taken seriously as a critical reflection of the state of education of young people, and schools in particular' (1991: 1). A key theme of Adams' book is that the root cause of most of the protests, demonstrations and riots that have occurred has been the authoritarian and repressive nature of schooling which he regards as a form of social violence committed against pupils in itself (Adams 1991: 62). Ironically, as he also points out, for a great deal of the history of British formal education, any protest by pupils at the level of social injustice inherent in authoritarian school and classroom organisation would be met with physical violence in the form of corporal punishment.

Sometimes, it is the inefficiency of authoritarian school structures that can cause violence. I have argued elsewhere in relation to a number of countries in Africa (Harber 1989: 124–126; Harber and Dadey 1991: 15–16) that violent riots often occur in African schools when the authoritarian school structures which pupils are supposed to depend and rely on, break down and things go wrong in contexts where there are often resource shortages of all kinds and where teachers are poorly paid, if at all, and thus have more than one job. This is not a situation that has gone away. A teacher in Zambia was recently quoted as saying 'From time to time there are problems: pupils run riot, disrupt learning and destroy property. If they are hungry they may attack the teachers' (Young 2002: 10). The basic problem is that strict hierarchies often mean that principals and staff do not communicate sufficiently with pupils. This poor communication leads to misunderstanding and generates suspicion. When things go wrong – allowances do not turn up, classes are left untaught, food is short, examination papers fail to appear – no explanation is forthcoming because there is no expectation that there should be one. Complaints are met with high-handedness and resentment grows among pupils anxious about their own futures until a small incident sparks off violence which has included serious attacks on personnel and buildings. African schools are not alone in this either. Despite a very different resource context, one researcher in France argues that his evidence suggests that rising levels of violence in French schools are partly due to a feeling amongst the pupils that the system is against them and a key factor in this is poor school organisation and management (Marshall 2000).

Abello (1997) uses evidence from Colombia to argue that the authoritarian nature of schooling is not only a form of violence itself, often causing violent reactions in school, but also helps to sow the seeds of violence in the wider society. She argues that the school teaches the seeds of non-co-existence through its authoritarianism, rigidity, uniformity, vertical hierarchies and its denial or repression of the emotions, feelings, desires, interests, likes and dislikes of pupils as these are not essential to the functioning of the school. Pupils do not learn how to communicate and relate to each other or to authority in ways that favour peaceful coexistence, creative and cooperative problem solving and conflict resolution. Hence,

> The school, which is the cradle of democracy because it is the natural home of reason and discussion, is failing in its purpose because of dogma, knowledge imparted in an authoritarian manner and blind faith in the written word, absolute, final truths, unique explanations and preconceived ideas, leading to a rejection of diverse explanation of reality. In this way, it aggravates society's backwardness and no wonder that violence ensues.
>
> (Abello 1997: 463)

A note on school size

Authoritarian school organisation can be exacerbated by the scale of schooling. Connections between mass schooling, mass production, social control and authoritarianism, discussed in more detail in Chapter 4, are perhaps at their clearest in the common phenomenon of the large school, particularly at the secondary level. Large schools have often been described as factory-like in the way that students are treated as products. Such large-scale schooling requires a particular degree of bureaucratised and regimented control and order that has worrying results,

> Bigness in schools was and is deliberate, originally a policy response to the stated needs of the captains of industry, the builders of factories. Big schools tend to be mechanistic and managerial, hierarchical and bureaucratic. Everyone does the same tasks in the same way, like miniaturised factory workers or little soldiers. Whilst all kids are different, in big schools those differences usually make no difference; youngsters are treated as if they are interchangeable, even expendable. Big, comprehensive, competitive schools worked for some and failed for many others. Too many students alienated from schools, disconnected from education . . . dropout rates, suicides and instances of violence are all higher in big schools.
>
> (Ayers 2000: 4)

As we have seen, there is long-standing evidence of student dissatisfaction with schooling, particularly secondary schooling. Fullan's survey of 3600 students in schools in Canada found widespread evidence of what they called 'the alienation theme'. Students were consistently critical of a lack of communication, dialogue, participation and engagement in the process of learning. Generally, the students exhibited little sense of identity or belonging (Fullan 1991: 171). This evidence of alienation and its attendant social dangers has been linked to forms of mass organisation, including schooling,

> Within the mass world of modern times, small groups do exist and thrive, but the overall intimacy has been lost, while personal isolation has become a constant risk for individuals. A scan of the human scene overall shows clearly that the quality of personal lives and the values of the social milieu are intricately interrelated, while both are conditioned by the degree of social intimacy that exists. This indicates that intimacy, not social massing, is the right climate for fostering human development and formative education. Hence the relationship that is found everywhere between expanding community size and social/personal degeneration: crime, alcoholism, drugs, stress, neurosis, loneliness and all the other outcomes of depersonalised mass society.
>
> (Hemming 1991: 8)

Supporters of small schools, on the other hand, while recognising that it is perfectly possible to have oppressive small schools, nevertheless argue that smaller schools can more easily facilitate the creation of a more democratic, inclusive and responsible environment (Harber 1996: 40–41, 49). It is also argued that the familiarity of strong, personal, and face-to-face relationships drastically reduces the risk of alienation and isolation fostered by the impersonality of large schools and hence reduces the risk of crime and violence. As one British headteacher put it,

> Parents have long been suspicious of the large school. They fear its anonymity. Most meetings in corridors are encounters with strangers. Pupils will do things when they are not known, to people whom they do not know, far more readily than they would to those whom they do know.
>
> (Anderson 1991: 13)

Esteve quotes evidence that problems of violence are considerably worse in schools with a large number of pupils which 'suggests that the impersonal nature of the large institutions contributes to deterioration in interpersonal relations and the feelings of self-esteem of the pupils. Their frustration may be expressed as violence towards inanimate objects (vandalism) or towards a teacher' (2000: 206). Indeed, Klonsky (2000) has linked the killings in Columbine High School, Colorado in 1999 and other such killings in the USA to the anomie of big schools and the consequent lack of connection between educator and student. In America, school size has increased fivefold since 1945 and student populations of 2000–5000 are not uncommon. Yet there is evidence that small schools and schools-within-a-school can have a considerable impact in reducing school violence (Ayers *et al.* 2000).

Conclusion

This chapter has argued that the dominant or hegemonic model of schooling internationally is authoritarian. Pupils have little say in how schools are run, what is taught or how it is taught and this situation is perhaps at its most pronounced in large schools. It is this authoritarianism that provides the context for schools' role in the reproduction and perpetration of violence. In the light of this analysis the next chapter begins to explore ways in which schooling is involved in violence towards young people.

3   Schooling and violence

When children are trained, they learn how to train others in turn. Children who are lectured to, learn how to lecture; if they are admonished, they learn how to admonish; if scolded, they learn how to scold; if ridiculed, they learn how to ridicule; if humiliated, they learn how to humiliate; if their psyche is killed, they will learn how to kill.

(Miller 1987: 98)

Introduction

Despite concern about violence by pupils on pupils and pupils on teachers in schools it is important to remember that, as the Gulbenkian Foundation pointed out, 'In general, children are far more often victims of violence than perpetrators' and that 'Schools can either be a force for violence prevention, or can provide an experience which reinforces violent attitudes and adds to the child's experience of violence' (1995: 1, 139). Yet,

When we respond to violence in schools, if we respond at all, it is to the children who are violent. When a child forces another to do his or her bidding, we call it extortion; when an adult does the same thing to a child, it is called correction. When a student hits another student it is assault; when a teacher hits a student it is for the child's 'own good'. When a student embarrasses, ridicules or scorns another student it is harassment, bullying or teasing. When a teacher does it, it is sound pedagogical practice.

(Ross Epp 1996: 20)

It has been argued by Abello (1997) that this dimension of the relationship between schooling and violence, that schooling can be a form of violence against children, has received insufficient academic attention and that it 'is a problem that has been little studied – its very existence denied' while it seems to attract a low level of interest 'judging from the scant documentation and discussion among educational researchers'. Abello argues that this lack of interest results from a number of factors. First, a blind spot among educational researchers which is a refusal to see the violence which education may be reproducing from society or the violence it helps to generate within the education system. An interesting example of this is Robin Alexander's otherwise immensely detailed study of culture and pedagogy across five nations (Alexander 2000) which won the American Educational Research Association's outstanding book award for 2002. One of the five countries studied is India where corporal punishment is widely used in schools and classrooms yet no mention is made of this in the book. Even books on schooling and violence tend to ignore or play down school to pupil violence. For example, an international and comparative study of violence at school published by UNESCO does acknowledge that the authoritarian nature of schooling can contribute to pupil violence but has little on violence done to pupils (Oshako 1997: 14, 37). A recent book on violence in schools in Europe noted that only two of the seventeen countries surveyed (Germany and Ireland) had reported on teacher to pupil violence. The German chapter commented that 'Investigation of violence used by teachers against pupils is not possible in Germany because the authority which must approve such investigations is at the same time the proper authority of the teachers' (Smith 2003: 6). An Israeli commentary on the European chapters noted this gap in the book and commented,

> We find this gap in the literature quite disturbing. Although corporal punishment is explicitly prohibited in most if not all European countries, the issue of maltreatment by school staff should not be neglected. There is a sharp contrast between the significant negative ramifications of physical and emotional maltreatment by adults who are expected to protect the pupil and the little attention to this area . . . Our studies in Israel strongly suggest that victimisation (especially emotional) by staff is not negligible in prevalence.
>
> (Benbenishty and Astor 2003: 238–239)

Second, a conceptual limitation of school violence which makes it difficult to address the issue in any serious or systematic way. Third, a tendency in the school system for 'ought' to come before 'is' and for it to have an idealised, taken-for-granted image as inherently good and beneficial.

This book sets out to begin to balance this situation by exploring in a systematic manner and in some detail the other side of the coin – the violence carried out against learners by schooling systems. It is important to stress that the intention is very definitely not to blame any group such as teachers or educational administrators for this violence but to explore what it is about schooling *as a system* that can lend itself to a violent and oppressive interpretation. While there are incidences of malicious violence by teachers, 'systemic violence' is often the consequence of taken-for-granted, 'common-sense' assumptions that existing pedagogical approaches and educational practices are necessarily in the best interests of pupils

(Ross Epp 1996: 1). Teachers and administrators are often victims of systems in the same way that pupils are. However, it is nevertheless vital to explore what it is about schooling as a system that can lend itself to violent interpretation in the hope that understanding what is bad in the social construction of schooling will help in the creation and expansion of what is good in education in general.

Schooling and the causes of violence

What are we to understand by the term 'violence' and its relationship to education? Schostack (1986: Ch. 2) provides a useful and detailed discussion of different ways of explaining why violence occurs. He divides these into three broad groups – biological, psychological and criminological/sociological. Whether or not one accepts that there are biological, instinctive tendencies towards violence inherent in human beings, different rates of violence between different individuals and cultural groups in similar contexts and between the same individual and cultural groups in different contexts strongly suggests that the conditions of human existence – the social structures and cultural practices and relationships that shape our lives – must influence whether or not we behave violently. As the Gulbenkian Foundation's report on children and violence, which looks in detail at why children become violent, said in relation to gender, 'Violence is overwhelmingly a male problem, and the roots for this appear to be primarily social rather than biological, highlighting the inadequacies of current socialisation of male children . . .' (1995: 11).

Indeed, the authoritative 1986 Seville Statement on Violence signed by twenty scientists from such fields as animal behaviour, psychology, sociology, neurophysiology, genetics and biochemistry – adopted by UNESCO in 1989 – rejected a biological basis to human violence and war altogether. They argued that biological explanations had been misused to justify violence, for example, that the theory of evolution had been used to justify not only war but also genocide, colonialism and suppression of the weak. They stated their position in the form of five propositions (which are more elaborated in the original):

- It is scientifically incorrect to say that we have inherited a tendency to make war from our animal ancestors.
- It is scientifically incorrect to say that war or any other violent behaviour is genetically programmed into our human nature.
- It is scientifically incorrect to say that in the course of human evolution there has been a selection for aggressive behaviour more than other kinds of behaviour.
- It is scientifically incorrect to say that humans have a 'violent brain'.
- It is scientifically incorrect to say that war is caused by 'instinct' or any single motivation.

They concluded that, 'biology does not condemn humanity to war . . . just as "wars begin in the minds of men", peace also begins in our minds' (UNESCO, 1989).

Here I am going to discuss briefly two closely interconnected social/ psychological explanations of the causes of violent behaviour in relation to socialisation which are relevant to the authoritarian role of schooling in reproducing and perpetrating violence.

The first is the idea of role modelling, that is if those adults who young people are expected by society to admire, respect and imitate are consistently authoritarian to them they will come to accept this as the normal way of relating to others – giving orders or taking orders. Similarly, if those in authority over them are physically violent and abusive towards them, then this becomes normal for them and they will reproduce this violence in their own relationships with others. In other words they become socialised through imitation into authoritarianism, repression and violent means to achieve ends. The psychoanalyst Alice Miller has written convincingly about the authoritarian roots of violence in child-rearing, driven partly by her need to understand how leading Nazis could have behaved in the way that they did. She states that she was unable to find a single figure amongst the leading Nazis who did not have a strict, rigid and authoritarian upbringing. Indeed, her book *For Your Own Good* begins with a telling quote. Rudolph Hess, Commandant at the Auschwitz concentration camp, said,

> It was constantly impressed upon me in forceful terms that I must obey promptly the wishes and commands of my parents, teachers and priests, and indeed of all grown-up people, including servants, and that nothing must distract me from this duty. Whatever they said was always right. These basic principles by which I was brought up became second nature to me.
>
> (Miller 1987: xxiii)

Miller analyses what she terms the 'poisonous pedagogy' of doing harm to children while using a language that purports to be doing them good. Miller argues that the poisonous pedagogy of the role models of parents and teachers imparts to the child from the beginning beliefs about behaviour and relationships that have been passed on from generation to generation even though they are false. Some of these as outlined by Miller are:

- Children are undeserving of respect simply because they are children.
- Obedience makes a child strong.
- A high degree of self-esteem is harmful.
- A low degree of self-esteem makes a person altruistic.
- Tenderness is harmful.

- Severity and coldness (including corporal punishment) are a good preparation for life.

(Miller 1987: 59–60)

A former CIA psychiatrist studying the former Iraqi leader Saddam Hussein, traces the roots of his dictatorial violence to a history of rejection by his mother and a physically and psychologically brutal and abusive upbringing by his stepfather (Borger 2002). While all children who are treated in such a manner do not go on to be political dictators because there are often countervailing and modifying socialisation influences, and because they don't have the opportunity, serious damage can be done to individuals and the results can negatively affect societies in other lower-level, everyday ways through such manifestations of violence as bullying, harassment, racism, sexual violence and crime. It is interesting to note that in the Cambridge study of Delinquent Development the biggest difference between the violent offenders and non-violent frequent offenders was in parental authoritarianism, with the violent offenders having more authoritarian parents (Gulbenkian Foundation 1995: 48).

The second, related idea is that authoritarianism and its emphasis on automatic obedience to orders is very dangerous as it conditions and permits individuals to carry out violent acts by proving a justification or legitimation for them – 'I was only obeying orders'. Many individual acts of violence have been carried out and justified in the name of the duty to obey. Milgram's experiments using ordinary people to carry out what they thought were acts of violence against others simply because the authority said that it was necessary indicated that behaviour similar to that of officials in Nazi Germany could be replicated in American citizens. The experiment involved two people: an actor playing the part of a student trying to remember different words and the other – the real subject – playing the role of the teacher. The subject was told to give the student an electric shock every time he missed a word and increase the voltage as he got more answers wrong. They had no idea that the shouting and writhing of the 'students' were not real but in many cases went on to administer the shocks to dangerous levels when pressed by their instructor. Before the experiments it was predicted that about 1 per cent would obey the order to use violence whereas incidences between 33 per cent and 50 per cent were recorded (Milgram 1971). As Professor Philip Zimbardo of Stanford University, who carried out similar experiments using 'prisoner'/'guard' roles, said in a recent film on the origins of violent tyranny, 'more crimes are committed in the name of obedience than disobedience. It is those who follow any authority blindly who are the real danger' (Bright 2000).

Of course, in an authoritarian setting with an expectation of obedience, with low levels of concern for social justice and with no other ways of dealing with dissent or difference, then individuals or groups who reject what is happening to them may well resort to physical violence because there is no other way to respond or because they have learned that this is the normal way to behave and respond. As we saw in the previous chapter, violence may be an inevitable reaction to violent structures. Students in Canada, for example, were asked in focus groups to identify what it was about schools that made them angry. Students listed hundreds of things that made them angry but at the crux of the matter were power relationships and matters of equity (Ross Epp 1996: 8). Many of the aspects of these two explanations for the causes of violence discussed above have been, and still can be, found in the organisation, values and practices of formal schooling.

Types of violence in education

The central focus of the present book is on violence as is understood in the direct manner of the Gulbenkian Foundation's Commission on Children and Violence – 'Violence is defined as behaviour by people against people liable to cause physical or psychological harm' (1995: 4). The World Health Organization defines violence as, 'The intentional use of physical force or power, threatened or actual, against oneself, another person, or against a group or community, that either results in or has a high likelihood of resulting in, injury, death, psychological harm, maldevelopment or deprivation' (WHO 2002: 5).

The inclusion of the word 'power' expands the conventional understanding of violence to include those acts that result from a power relationship, including threats and intimidation – it also serves to include neglect or acts of omission in addition to the more obvious acts of commission.

The veteran peace researcher Johan Galtung has pointed out that no universally accepted typology of violence exists and that no two researchers use the same definition (Galtung 1981: 13). However, Salmi (1999) has provided a useful categorisation of four types of violence that can be applied to schools:

1 His first category is *direct violence* – deliberate injury to the integrity of human life. This includes murder, massacre, genocide, torture, rape, maltreatment, forced resettlement, kidnapping, forced labour and slavery.
2 *Indirect violence* is the indirect violation of the right to survival. This is violence by omission or lack of protection against poverty, hunger, disease, accidents, natural catastrophes or is mediated violence through harmful modifications to the environment.
3 *Repressive violence* is the deprivation of fundamental human rights such as freedom of thought, freedom of religion, freedom of speech, right to a fair trial, equality before the law, freedom of movement and the freedom to vote.

4 *Alienating violence* or the deprivation of higher rights consists of alienating working conditions, racism (and presumably sexism), social ostracism, cultural repression and living in fear.

All four types of violence can be found in formal schooling and are discussed in more detail in subsequent chapters of this book. Indirect, repressive and alienating violence as defined above contribute to a context which increases the possibility and occurrence of direct forms of violence in schools.

While the role of formal schooling in causing and reproducing direct violence constitutes the central focus of this book, alienating violence (e.g. racism or sexism) is often a major cause of, and factor determining the nature of, the physical violence that takes place in the school and which the school helps to reproduce in the wider society. Schools and racism are discussed further in Chapter 6 and schools and gendered violence are discussed further in Chapter 7. It is also possible to place stress and anxiety in this category as they are caused by the extreme working conditions of competition and testing in schools and lead to the physical harm of children. This is discussed further in Chapter 8.

Repressive violence, or authoritarianism as it is termed in this book, is common in schools, part of which is Bourdieu's 'symbolic violence' of schools imposing forms of politically dominant knowledge (Grenfell and James 1998: 24–25). This was discussed in Chapter 2. It is this authoritarian educational context which both necessitates and allows for direct violence to take place in the form of physical punishment (Chapter 5) and which allows racism and sexism to happen and be perpetuated. Indeed, the authoritarian nature of schooling has sometimes led to the use of military metaphors in describing school philosophy and organisation. Chapter 9 argues that the relationship can be more than a metaphor with schooling being directly involved in military training and preparation for violence.

Salmi's final category, indirect violence or violence by omission or default occurs when schools fail to provide protection against something. This is not an explicit theme of subsequent chapters which concentrate on how and why schools are more directly violent towards pupils. However, it is a significant aspect of schooling so the remainder of this chapter will discuss how schools can and are involved in violence by omission.

Violence by omission

As we saw in Chapters 1 and 2, children and young people are encouraged, persuaded and even forced to attend school by national governments and international agencies, even though schooling may not automatically or uniformly be beneficial for them and they may be reluctant to do so. However, school may actually be harmful if, having got them there, it fails to protect children from violence and suffering when it could do so. Indeed, they could be in danger simply by entering the school building. When an earthquake shook the town of San Giuliano di Puglia in southern Italy in November 2002 the sole building it completely destroyed was the local primary school, killing 26 children and a teacher. It became clear that the school had been cheaply and poorly built despite a history of earthquakes in the region. The final date for making all school buildings secure had been put back five times because of a lack of funds. Since the earthquake a number of surveys and reports have come to light suggesting that around half the schools in Italy are unsafe or lacking safety certification (Willan 2002; Newbold 2002, 2003). A government report in Japan, where tremors are common, revealed that less than half of all schools and universities are sufficiently earthquake resistant. Some experts have predicted that a force 6 or 7 earthquake will hit the Kanto region soon in which case half of Tokyo's schools would simply disintegrate. Moreover, two thirds of the schools in Tokyo have no nearby evacuation spaces. Boards of education have repeatedly asked for money to re-build schools to make them safe but it has not been provided (Fitzpatrick 2003). In KwaZulu Natal, South Africa, almost a quarter of schools were reported as being unfit for educational purposes and most of these were considered too dangerous to be occupied by pupils because of the precarious state of the buildings (Maloney 1997). In England the Community Practitioners' and Health Visitors' Association are to investigate the state of school toilets as they are concerned that many are unhygienic and are breeding grounds for germs which could affect the health and well-being of pupils (*Times Educational Supplement* 29/1/2002). In Russia the Prime Minister ordered an immediate fire survey of all schools following the death of 28 children in southern Russia following another fire three days before in Siberia where 22 children died. Prosecutors blamed the high death toll in Siberia on building code violations including a blocked fire escape. Russia's *Izvestia* newspaper reported that in 2002, 700 fires damaged school buildings across Russia (Mollayev 2003).

A central thesis of this book is that it is the authoritarian nature of much of schooling that provides the context for direct forms of violence and that this in turn is based on a key and dominant purpose in its historical origins and international development – the perceived need and desire to survey, regulate and control. This is more fully discussed in the next chapter. It might seem paradoxical, therefore, that the present section is arguing that schools can also be responsible for violence because they do not survey, regulate and control *enough*, that is that schools ignore violence in their midst or potential threats from outside and therefore fail to protect their children. Yet this violence by omission happens for reasons consistent with the authoritarian basis of direct violence. First, it can happen because schools explicitly or tacitly condone the type of violence that is happening and therefore do not intervene to stop it. Second, education personnel simply may not recognise it as an issue because it is so much part of their common-sense understanding of how the world 'is' and it is therefore perceived as 'natural' and 'inevitable'. Third, schools are reluctant to intervene or find it difficult to do so because the type of intervention required is not congruent with what are perceived as the main purposes of the authoritarian type of education often provided – the teacher-centred transmission of largely cognitive curriculum content, whether this is 'factual' knowledge, understanding of concepts or basic skills. Schools and teachers are often ill-equipped and unwilling to deal with controversial issues, values and with the affective dimension of learning – feelings, emotions and relationships. Teachers' own education and training has often not emphasised the importance of these, yet to be able to handle them effectively would require a transformation of school and classroom power relationships in a significantly more democratic direction. Schools therefore regularly find themselves implicated in indirect violence by omission.

The following themes and examples of violence by omission, as with direct violence later in the book, are necessarily selective and no claim is made that each one occurs everywhere. However, a sufficiently wide range of evidence of all types of school violence exists in a sufficiently wide range of national contexts and cultures to be able to ask serious questions about why and how schools are allowed to be implicated in violence at all.

Bullying

Bullying can take many forms – physical violence, threats, name-calling, sarcasm, spreading rumours, persistent teasing, exclusion from a group, tormenting, ridicule, humiliation and abusive comments. All are a form of violence. Teacher–pupil bullying certainly exists and will be discussed in Chapter 5. Pupil–pupil bullying is a common problem in schools internationally (Roland and Munthe 1989; Oshako 1997; Ruiz 1998). One study of 13-year-olds in 27 countries found that the majority had been engaged in bullying at least some of the time (WHO 2002: 29–30). This in itself is an indictment of schools' inability to eradicate it, given that pupils are compelled, cajoled and persuaded to attend. Though there are variations in the types of bullying perpetrated, bullying is carried out by both males and females and both males and females are the victims. However, ostensibly schools play no part in creating it and do their best to put an end to it – or do they? Biddulph (1998) points out that schools can play a large part in actually creating the problem of bullying. For example, lower achieving pupils, belittled in the competitive atmosphere, may strive to regain some dignity through bullying. He also points out that while school sport has the potential for learning team spirit, giving your best and shared endeavour, it can also exclude those who don't excel and it can become brutish with over-competitiveness, over-stressing the body and the promotion of aggression and violence.

Do schools then actively try to stop bullying? Evidence suggests that schools are implicated in violence by omission in relation to bullying.

A survey of 2772 pupils in Britain in 2000 reported that more than half the respondents had experienced bullying but just under half said their school did not have an anti-bullying policy, despite being required to do so since 1999. Of those with a policy only about half said they thought it was working. Commenting on the findings the authors note that during their research, headteachers told them that if you make a big thing out of bullying, parents will think you have a bullying problem in your school (Katz *et al.* 2001: Ch. 5). In a context of league tables and competition between schools, headteachers are under pressure to present the best face possible to the outside world and may well therefore be reluctant to have an overtly stated anti-bullying policy. However, teachers' leaders have also been reported as saying that it is unfair to expect schools to take responsibility for bullying, claiming that the problem stemmed from the upbringing of pupils (Smithers 2000a). Katz and colleagues (2001: Ch. 5) also note that some teachers bully others in the staffroom and therefore resist a whole school ethos change. They may well be correct about this. A survey of 5300 private and public sector workers suggested that teaching is one of the worst professions for workplace bullying. One in ten of those surveyed complained of being bullied in the past six months but the figure rose to 15.5 per cent for teachers. Over the last five years the figures were 24.2 per cent for all workers but 35.4 per cent for teachers. The report suggested that many school managers did not have the training to cope with their jobs and workloads and resorted to bullying to control their staff (Thornton 2000). A survey of 2000 teachers and lecturers found that more than half were victims of bullying. In more than half the reported cases headteachers were identified as the people responsible (Stewart 2003). A survey of 241 teacher trainees carried out by King's College London found that 43 per cent of trainees reported feeling bullied in school while on teaching practice placement and 18 per cent reported feeling bullied in their colleges. Women under 28 were particularly affected. Some of the bullies were trainees' tutors but most were school mentors. While some students confronted their mentors successfully, others went to the college for support only to be told to grin and bear it (R. Klein 2000).

In Japan in 2001 a court in Yokohama ordered an education authority to pay £232,000 to the parents of a boy who killed himself as a result of bullying in 1994 because the school had failed to act to protect him. In 2000 an estimated 339 students committed suicide because they were being bullied by classmates. As the article that reported this commented, 'A spate of civil actions by parents against school authorities and alleged victimisation in the past decade have highlighted the view that schools are not doing enough to discourage bullying' (Fitzpatrick 2001). In Greece a survey of 1312 pupils in the greater Athens area reported that relatively few of the victimised pupils sought the help of the teacher, suggesting that most of them did not feel comfortable talking about their experience to teachers. The study speculated that they may fear being labelled 'victims', 'cowards' or 'inadequate' and thus risk further bullying or they may feel that nothing can be done about it (Houndoumadi and Peteraki 2001: 25). In Australia, the government is introducing new laws to force schools to tackle bullying. Studies have found that one child in six is bullied each week in Australian schools and that 50 per cent of children have been bullied in the last year. Only 36 per cent of new teachers recently surveyed felt that their course adequately addressed how to deal with bullying (Masien 2003).

A particular type of bullying that has received more attention in recent years is homophobic bullying. In Canada in 2002, for example, the British Columbia human rights tribunal ruled that a school board discriminated against a pupil by failing to protect him against homophobic bullying in school. Over three years he was spat upon, repeatedly punched, verbally abused and on one occasion had his shirt set on fire. The tribunal ordered every school board in the province to put in place programmes to deal with harassment based on sexual orientation. The president of the British Columbia School Trustees Association thought this issue would now have to be faced by school boards across the whole of Canada (Greenfield 2002). In Britain there is widespread evidence of homophobic bullying at school and the failure of schools to deal with the problem adequately (Mason and Palmer 1996). Berliner (2001) quotes research that suggests that 46,000 secondary school pupils are being bullied for their sexual orientation and that over half of young gay men and lesbian women have considered suicide because of homophobic bullying while 40 per cent have actually tried to kill themselves and three quarters of this group have attempted suicide more than once. In a survey of 1177 sixth formers, the overwhelming majority of whom were heterosexual, 43 per cent said their school was either not a safe place for gay pupils or only sometimes safe. Parallel interviews with 15 gay young people suggested that teachers were reluctant to deal with homophobia, with some teachers afraid of being called gay by pupils if they confronted the bullies (Mansell 2002). In America, New York City is set to open its first state school for gay, lesbian and bisexual students because of a severe rise of cases of harassment and assault – a survey found that 70 per cent of gay and lesbian students in New York faced verbal, physical, sexual or physical harassment or assault at school (Goffe 2003). In these examples schools are failing to protect pupils from homo-phobic bullying, despite official political condemnation of such behaviour. In some countries, however, homophobic bullying would seem to be encouraged right from the very top. In Zimbabwe, Robert Mugabe has frequently expressed the view that homosexuals are 'worse than pigs' and 'have no rights at all' (McGreal 2002) while in Namibia President Sam Nujoma has described homosexuality as a 'hideous deviation of decrepit and inhuman sordid behaviour' which should be 'totally uprooted' (*Mail and Guardian* February 14–20 1997).

HIV/AIDS

This is now a global pandemic with infection rates increasing particularly rapidly in southern Africa, India, China, Indonesia, the Russian Federation and Ukraine. It is no exaggeration to say that in some societies it is reaching the point of seriously threatening economic and social collapse (Bosely 2002). Education is potentially the most important factor in preventing the further spread of HIV/AIDS. Yet schooling can contribute directly and indirectly to the spread of HIV/AIDS. As Michael Kelly of the University of Zambia has pointed out, in southern Africa school costs, the context of poverty and intense competition for academic success may lead to sexual relations with teachers, other adults and higher achieving fellow students. Long walking distances to and from school contribute to the risk of rape (cited in Vally 2001). The role of schooling in directly contributing to the sexual harm of pupils will be discussed more fully in Chapter 7 on schooling, violence and gender. Here the concern is with the school's indirect role. In all societies, but particularly in those where HIV/AIDS is widespread, if schools and teachers do not attempt to combat the spread of the disease then this is violence by omission. Inaction or ineffective action by the formal education system can result in the deaths of many pupils. A study of Pakistan, India, Uganda and Ghana for the Overseas Development Administration found that sex education was mentioned in textbooks but taught superficially and with considerable discomfort by teachers. Coverage of HIV/AIDS in the Asian countries was minimal and not related to sexual intercourse, though Ghana and Uganda provided more detail on sex education. Teaching methods in all four countries were primarily didactic (Barnett *et al.* 1995). A recent study of Kenya and Tanzania, two countries with high levels of HIV/AIDS infection, found that governments in both countries had been slow in using the education system to combat the spread of the disease and in Kenya in particular there had been a lack of political will in expressing a national commitment and providing overall leadership in response to the pandemic. There has also been resistance from religious groups in Kenya who prefer a simple 'no sex before marriage' approach. A survey of pupils found that the most common source of information about HIV/AIDS was the radio, followed by newspapers with school coming third. As the report comments, 'What is amazing is that the school is not a leading source of information' (Juma 2001: 38).

Teaching about HIV/AIDS requires a move away from an emphasis on the transmission of knowledge to discussing sensitive and controversial issues in the classroom as well as relationships and values. This in itself requires a change in the power structure of the classroom to one which is less teacher-led and where there is a greater emphasis of pupil participation and open dialogue. Despite their potential as an agency that could reach many young people the very nature of schools and the education systems of which they form a part often means that they are not well designed for this. Mirembe's research in Uganda, where considerable effort has been put into HIV/AIDS education, found that teachers put emphasis on control of pupils and the passing on of knowledge. Lessons were teacher-centred, denying young people a chance to produce knowledge and to be in charge of their learning. In line with Chapter 2 of this book she describes the school she witnessed as authoritarian with little exploration of values; an approach, she argues, that is unlikely to change behaviour even if knowledge is increased. The school also did little to try to challenge through discussion and interrogation dominant patterns of male-dominance and sexism in education and society, a major factor in the spread of HIV/AIDS. Condom use, for example, assumes partnership and negotiation. This situation was not helped by the national curriculum as HIV/AIDS education did not contribute significantly to grades and therefore was seen as a waste of time by teachers and pupils (Mirembe 2002). Again, it has been suggested in relation to Kenya and Tanzania that working outside the formal school setting with various youth clubs and religious groups is more productive because participants take part freely 'without any coercion' (Juma 2001: 10).

A major problem is that, because of the nature of schooling that they themselves have experienced and have been trained for, schoolteachers in many countries do not feel trained to teach about controversial issues and so avoid doing so. A survey of 679 teachers in Britain for example found that there was a reluctance to discuss controversial issues in the classroom (Davies *et al.* 1999). Re-training of teachers to teach about HIV/AIDS in Kenya and Tanzania has been 'sporadic and patchy' (Juma 2001: 79) while such a description could also be used for re-training in South Africa (Vally 2000; Tshoane 2001). There can also be individual and cultural resistance to the open and honest approaches required by sex education. The Minister of Education in South Africa, for example, said that,

> There are many teachers who are uncomfortable with issues of sex, sexuality, sexual preference and condoms. They prefer to take the easy way out, which is to say that HIV/AIDS will be halted when pupils 'behave' and practice abstinence and delayed sexual initiation.
>
> (Motala *et al.* 1999: 28)

Four days after this speech, at an in-service training session for 200 teachers who were given a talk on sexually transmitted diseases, half walked out because of the explicit nature of the slides. When the next lecturer spoke about contraception and sexual protection the remainder of the audience, except for about eight people, got up and left the hall. One of the few teachers that remained said, 'I couldn't believe it. How can we expect to teach our children about the realities of a national crisis when we want to ignore those realities ourselves' (Dyanti 1999).

Michael Kelly of the University of Zambia doubts whether existing forms of schooling are relevant in a world with HIV/AIDS. He contends that the entire content, process, methodology, role and organisation of schooling must be radically altered if it is going to deal effectively with the pandemic. This would involve incorporating aspects of non-formal education with the traditional school being replaced by a community based service organisation that would provide not only education but other services as well. This re-configuration would include among other things involving young people in programme design and delivery, with a firm focus of promoting peer education; using participatory methods and experiential learning techniques and developing a learning climate that firmly and frequently re-affirms the principles of respect, responsibility and rights (cited in Vally 2001).

Racism

The school's direct role in reproducing racism will be more fully discussed in Chapter 6. Here it is important to note briefly that schools also play an indirect role by ignoring or playing down issues of race and racism. One survey of racism in Europe carried out by the European Commission found that in 13 out of 15 countries a majority of people described themselves as either 'very racist', 'quite racist' or a 'little racist' (Dutter 1997). The exceptions were Portugal and Luxembourg, though in the context of Portugal at least, this has been challenged and described as the 'myth of Portuguese anti-racism' (Cardoso 1998). Indeed, across Europe racist right-wing parties have been rapidly growing in electoral strength since the end of the 1990s. In Britain there has been widespread and consistent evidence of significantly high levels of racism among the population in general and young people in particular (Cullingford 2000; Harber 2002a: 233–235). The most recent British Social Attitudes Survey, however, found that those who were willing to describe themselves as 'a little racially prejudiced' or 'very racially prejudiced' was down to an all time low of 25 per cent (Carvel 2002). While any decline should be welcomed, this survey, like the European Commission survey above, is based on self-description and is therefore likely to underestimate actual levels of racism as people may simply be less willing to admit to it. That a quarter of the British population is willing to admit to it is still worrying, especially in the light of a number of local electoral successes for the far-right and racist British National Party. A survey of overseas teachers in south-east England recently found high levels of racist abuse from pupils (Farrell 2003). A nation-wide survey of whites in America found that a majority said that they believed blacks and Hispanics are likely to prefer welfare to hard work and tend to be lazier than whites, more prone to violence, less intelligent and less patriotic (Landry 1997: 56). No genuine education worthy of its name in America, Europe in general or in Britain could result in this situation so either schooling is trying very hard but failing, which would raise serious questions about the worth of schooling as a form of expensive public investment, or it has not been trying anything like hard enough. The second is more likely. In the same way that teachers are often reluctant to discuss controversial sexual issues in the classroom as a result of the nature of their own education and training, so they are often reluctant to confront controversial political issues like racism. Indeed, in some countries the curriculum might make this very difficult anyway. A summary of six research projects by the government funded Economic and Social Research Council on 16–19-year-olds in the mid-1980s found considerable political innocence, naivety and ignorance among young people coupled with 'endemic' racism – not the hallmarks of a healthy multiracial democracy, as the study commented. However, many of the young people conceded that with greater knowledge they would not necessarily have reached racist conclusions and expressed regret that they had not been taught more about politics in school. The report concluded that,

> Lacking any political education in the broadest sense, young people will continue to exist in a condition of ignorance in which simple solutions, especially racist ones, will have appeal. This is not necessarily because of their intrinsic attractiveness but because of a perceived lack of alternatives. Some of the respondents in the present study seemed aware of this danger and wanted the sort of information that would prevent them from being drawn into racist simplicities. The policy implications are clear. The current reluctance to introduce political studies into the school curriculum needs to be re-evaluated.
>
> (McGurk 1987: 51)

Ironically, this report was published the year the then Conservative government published its proposals for a national curriculum which deliberately excluded the study of the social sciences, including politics. The introduction of 'citizenship education' into British schools is only likely to have a limited impact in this regard because of the wider educational context into which it is being introduced (Harber 2002a). As one writer on multiculturalism and ethnicity in England put it in relation to the need for citizenship education to actively promote a new global cosmopolitanism, teachers 'are either too tired or too terrified to take up this challenge' (Alibhai-Brown 2000).

Teachers in Germany are often at a loss to know how to deal with neo-Nazis who comprise 10 per cent of all pupils, according to Germany's internal intelligence agency, the Office for the Protection of the Constitution. Teachers are reluctant to confront the issue and many teachers in the former East Germany see xenophobic comments as young people exercising 'freedom of expression' after years of communist rule. Some teachers even commented that the neo-Nazis were often the more disciplined boys because of the militaristic nature of the groups they were in (Sharma 2001a).

A study of friendship patterns in multiracial schools in Malaysia (Malay, Chinese and Indian pupils) found that the predominant pattern was that pupils from different backgrounds did not mix and that pupils used racial distinctions extensively in their relationships. One important reason for this was that schools and teachers were not actively intervening in order to try to improve relations and promote positive interaction among pupils from different racial backgrounds. The net result was that schooling helps to reproduce the racial separation, mistrust and hostility of the wider society by omission (Santhiram 1995). Similar arguments could be made for the segregated education system in Northern Ireland where survey evidence revealed that young people from the Catholic and Protestant communities knew very little of each other and had few opportunities to interact (Dunn and Morgan 1999).

Research on successful black students in Alberta, Canada suggested among other things that schooling failed to protect them from name calling, racial hostility and slurs and that they were subject to lower teacher expectations than white students and that this supported a number of other studies in Canada. Schools have committed a 'sin of omission by failing to incorporate black people's history and experiences into the curriculum'. The author quotes Giroux (1986: 10) to the effect that 'the issue here is that the school actively silences students by ignoring their histories . . . by refusing to provide them with the knowledge relevant to their lives' (Codjoe 2001).

A final example is South Africa where forty years of officially sanctioned institutionalised racism only ended in 1994. While some school desegregation has taken place in post-apartheid South Africa, a study of 90 schools across all nine provinces by the South African Human Rights Commission in the late 1990s showed conclusively that racism was still pervasive in schools. The report of the study commented that,

> Educators exhibit little or no commitment to constructing a learning environment free from discrimination and prejudice. Too many prefer to deny the existence of racism or presume a superficial tolerance. Some prefer to have their schools as laboratories for cultural assimilation where black learners are by and large tolerated rather than affirmed as of right. Four years after the miracle of 1994, school playgrounds are battlegrounds between black and white schoolgoers.
>
> (Vally and Dalamba 1999: Preface)

When students were asked 'Have there been racial incidents or examples of racism in your school?', 62 per cent answered yes. Almost 60 per cent of learners felt that their school did not have a policy/programme to eliminate racism or that it was unsuccessful (Vally and Dalamba 1999).

Gendered sexual violence

This can include various forms of sexual harassment – verbal sexual aggression, the threat of sexual abuse, unsolicited physical contact and enforced sexual interference. The underlying authoritarian and patriarchal context of direct sexual violence in schooling and its role in reproducing hegemonic forms of violent masculinity will be more fully discussed in Chapter 7. Here the purpose is to examine how schools can reproduce such violence by omission.

A study of the violence experienced by pupils at five junior high schools in America found that not only was bullying common but that 25 per cent of the female pupils had experienced sexual harassment at the hands of male students. The pupils said that teachers did not notice or ignored the violence experienced by the pupils. Administrators at the schools perceived violence to be less of a problem than the pupils and felt that teachers were more aware of the problem than pupils thought they were (MacDonald 1996). In England, one book on working with adolescent boys argued that,

> Secondary schools are often heavily gendered institutions with male-dominated cultures. These cultures are frequently made up of paternalistic leadership styles, competitive hierarchies, an over-emphasis on success, individualism, performance and getting ahead. White, middle-class, heterosexual men mainly hold power in our schools and they sometimes block change from taking place because they are power and gender blind about their own taken-for-granted positions and social relationships. . . . What is often being brushed under the carpet about boy's behaviour in schools, are the ritual insults, jeering, sexist jokes and name-calling made against girls and put-down of boys; the touching up and sexual harassment of girls, sexist graffiti, the sexual teasing; the bullying and psychological intimidation of girls and marginalized boys . . .
>
> (Salisbury and Jackson 1996: 11)

Discussion of evidence in the British context can be found in Jones (1985) and Mahoney (1985), both cited by Salisbury and Jackson.

Leach (2002) makes the point that studies of girls' under-representation in schooling in developing countries traditionally looked at factors external to the school (e.g. poverty, distance to school, early marriage) but ignored what happens inside schooling that might put girls off attending. This problem seems particularly serious in Africa. A study of Uganda found that sexual harassment of female pupils by male pupils is a common practice in schools but that it is ignored by teachers and governing boards. Neither female students nor female teachers reported sexual harassment. In some ways sexual harassment was seen as 'normal', inevitable and difficult to challenge (Mirembe and Davies 2001). Leach's own research in

Zimbabwe, Ghana and Malawi also found that sexual harassment, including physically violent harassment, of girls was widespread and that girls were again reluctant to report cases of sexual violence,

> This may have been through lack of confidence, absence of a support system or fear. Fear of further violence and reprisals, knowledge that they were unlikely to get sympathy and support from teachers or parents, a desire not to draw attention to oneself, and a certain resignation, an acceptance that this was how things were, all contributed to a lack of response. Girls seem to have been taught that they were always at fault; there was a general reluctance to blame males. In all three countries there was a depressing lack of trust in teachers expressed by pupils and few appeared to seek their advice, even from those teachers responsible for guidance and counselling.
>
> (Leach 2002: 10)

This reluctance to report matters to teachers is not surprising given that, as we shall see in Chapter 7, in these countries it is often teachers themselves who are to blame for the sexual harassment and sexual abuse of female pupils. Moreover, as Leach argues, it is the very authoritarian nature of schooling in many African schools which allows gender violence to flourish. In Kenya, Omale (2000) argues that negative attitudes towards girls permeate the classroom manifesting themselves in textbook content, the teaching/learning process and the peer culture. She cites the infamous incident at St Kizito School in northern Kenya in 1991 when 19 schoolgirls died and 71 were reportedly raped at the hands of their male peers. The headmaster commented that the boys had never meant to hurt the girls but 'only wanted to rape'. As Omale demonstrates, this was far from being an isolated incident. Pupils are reluctant to bring sexual harassment issues to the attention of teachers as they feel nothing will be done and because teachers themselves are deeply implicated. Again a connection is made with the authoritarian nature of schooling. Omale quotes Paul Ogula from the Department of Education at the Catholic University of Eastern Africa in Nairobi who argues that as long as some headteachers continue to run their schools as personal fiefdoms, the violence that characterises Kenyan schools will not end.

A similar situation exists in South Africa. The government appointed Gender Equity Task Team, reporting in 1997, stated that the South African education system was 'riddled with gender inequities' and that these included extremely worrying elements of sexual harassment and violence (Wolpe *et al.* 1997). In 2001 Human Rights Watch produced a report called *Scared at School* which documents in frightening detail violence against female pupils by male pupils. The report states,

The abuse girls experience at school is often magnified by the reactions they receive when they report abuse to school officials. Girls who did report abuse told Human Rights Watch that school officials responded with indifference, disbelief and hostility. Schools that do not take sexual violence and harassment seriously provide support for those who would commit violence against girls.

(Human Rights Watch 2001: 74)

Violence itself

This book is critical of the authoritarian nature of much mass schooling and of the violence that this gives rise to. However, John Devine in his book *Maximum Security: The Culture of Violence in Inner-City Schools* (1996) describes a situation in schools in New York, America where traditional forms of school authoritarianism have broken down but rather than being replaced with more constructive forms of democratic discipline and order have given way to a culture of violence. Educational staff have abdicated their responsibility for safety and security to an ineffective array of armed security guards who patrol the school and a technology of metal detectors, walkie-talkies and emergency security telephone systems in classrooms. Teachers focus purely on academic skills as defined by state-dictated curricular requirements and are not concerned with the whole student – behaviour, social skills and values. There is little insistence on personal responsibility and students conclude that teachers just do not care. As a result the schools he describes are a mixture of the trappings of repressive security technology masking a fundamentally *laisser-faire* culture in which half the pupils carry guns or knives and frequently use them. In this situation schooling, despite the obvious security presence, is failing to protect its pupils from violence.

South Africa also suffers from high levels of violence in schools in a situation where many schools do not function effectively (Harber 2001a: Ch. 4). A document resulting from an initiative of the Secretariat for Safety and Security and the Department of Education concluded that schools indirectly contributed to such violence because they failed to operate at the most basic level. In this way they opened 'space' for violence and failed to provide the basic sense of routine, support and security required for young people to develop and grow. In addition even those schools operating at a basic functional level continued to contribute to the system of violence because they do not address the risk factors underlying the system of violence, nor provide children with the tools of resilience. Schools contributed towards risk factors in the following ways:

- The authoritarian culture of the school and classroom management does not provide models for creative problem-solving, expression and conflict resolution.

- Schools fail to provide an alternative support unit in the context of high levels of family dysfunction.
- Schools fail to provide meaningful life-defining and reflective activities such as sport, arts and culture, story telling and discussion groups.
- Schools fail to provide children, or their families, with the qualities and skills needed to raise non-violent children.
- Schools fail to provide forums to process traumatic life experiences.
- Schools do not provide children with practical skills to access or create employment.
- Schools implicitly support patriarchy and concepts of hegemonic ('tough') masculinity for the male identity.

Schools also failed to provide tools of resilience in the following ways:

- Schools fail to provide a child with a strong sense of confidence with regards to schooling.
- Schools fail to provide additional support to children who encounter learning challenges. When a child stumbles in school, that child continues to fall.
- Schools fail to provide communication skills, decision-making skills or activities to formulate identity and self-esteem.
- Schools fail to provide a sense of confidence in the face of adversity.
- Schools fail to provide 'tools' to discover one's philosophical understanding of the world and 'place'.

(Porteous 1999: 15–16)

Conclusion

The root causes of violence are sociological as much as biological, if they are biological at all. Authoritarian forms of socialisation seem to play a major part in increasing the likelihood of violent behaviour through imitation and legitimation. This has serious implications for the nature of schooling as often currently constructed. Four types of violence were identified, all of which schools play a part in reproducing and perpetrating. However, schools don't necessarily have to be actively involved to reproduce violence – they can do this simply by ignoring violent threats to their pupils about which they could try to do something. This chapter has explored some of the ways in which schools are implicated in violence through omission.

4 Control, surveillance, reproduction and perpetration
Schools and inhuman capital theory

Schools have not necessarily much to do with education . . . they are mainly institutions of control where certain basic habits must be inculcated in the young. Education is quite different and has little place in school.

(Winston Churchill, cited in Shute 1992: 7)

There is nothing on earth intended for innocent people as horrible as a school. To begin with, it is a prison. But in some respects it is more cruel than a prison.

(George Bernard Shaw quoted in Meighan 1994)

We saw in Chapters 2 and 3 that schools are predominantly authoritarian institutions and that this provided the context for their role in perpetuating various forms of violence. Why are schools authoritarian? Why are the key international formal institutions of learning socially constructed in this way?

A history of education

Throughout the history of schooling there has always been a conflict between education for control in order to produce citizens and workers who were conformist, passive and politically docile on the one hand and those who wanted to educate for critical consciousness, individual liberation and participatory democracy on the other. It is the contention of this chapter that the former has dominated the real world of schooling, as opposed to educational debates and theory, because this was the main reason that formal, mass schooling systems were established in the first place and then expanded numerically and geographically. Some educational writers, practitioners and policy makers have championed the latter approach to schooling and education in general but the global persistence of the dominant authoritarian model suggests that the original purpose of control and compliance is deeply embedded in schooling and is highly resistant to change as a result. 'A band of efficient schoolmasters is kept at much less expense than a body of police or soldiery' (H. L. Bellairs, Victorian author of a report on the South Wales coalfield, cited in H. Williams 2003).

Green's historical study of the origins of formal schooling systems in England, France, the United States and Prussia in the nineteenth century argues that a key purpose of their construction was the formation and consolidation of national consciousness,

> The nineteenth century education system came to assume a primary responsibility for the moral, cultural and political development of the nation. It became the secular church. It was variously called upon to assimilate immigrant cultures, to promote established religious doctrines, to spread the standard form of the appointed national language, to forge a national identity and a national culture, to generalise new habits of routine and rational calculation, to encourage patriotic values, to inculcate moral disciplines and, above all, to indoctrinate in the political and economic creeds of the dominant classes. It helped construct the very subjectivities of citizenship, justifying the ways of the state to the people and the duties of the people to the state. It sought to create each person as a universal subject but it did so differentially according to class and gender. It formed the responsible citizen, the diligent worker, the willing tax payer, the reliable juror, the conscientious parent, the dutiful wife, the patriotic soldier and the dependable or deferential voter.
>
> (Green 1990: 80)

Schooling thus provided a means of social and political control, in particular to counter the threat to the state of increasingly industrialised, urbanised and potentially organised working populations. As Green's study argues, 'The task of public schooling was not so much to develop new skills for the industrial sector as to inculcate habits of conformity, discipline and morality that would counter the widespread problems of social disorder' (1990: 59). The Education Act of 1870 in England which established a quasi-national system of formal schooling 'was a result, as much as anything, of the desire to control the political effects of the extension of the franchise in 1867 to the skilled working class' (Green 1990: 33). Schooling would be organised to prepare future workers with the subordinate values and behaviours necessary for the modern bureaucratic, mass production workplace and the existing social order – regularity, routine, monotonous work and strict discipline. Its organisational form would therefore need to be authoritarian in order to inculcate habits of obedience and conformity. Two writers capture this relationship very well. Marten Shipman put it in his study of the history of education and modernisation,

> Punctuality, quiet orderly work in groups, response to orders, bells and timetables, respect for authority, even tolerance of monotony, boredom,

punishment, lack of reward and regular attendance at place of work are the habits to be learned at school.

(1971: 54–55)

Whereas Toffler argued that,

> Mass education was the ingenious machine constructed by industrialism to produce the kind of adults it needed . . . the solution was an educational system that, in its very structure, simulated this new world . . . the regimentation, lack of individualisation, the rigid systems of seating, grouping, grading and marking, the authoritarian style of the teacher – are precisely those that made mass public education so effective as an instrument of adaptation for its time and place.
>
> (1970: 354–355)

Indeed, not only were schools organised in an authoritarian manner to match the needs of the industrial workplace but, in England at least, were often extremely coercive and violent places as well, often being more punitive than the home (Adams 1991: 40).

Moreover, this authoritarianism was also reflected in the curriculum. Kelly (1986) argues that historically the dominant epistemology or view of knowledge that has influenced curriculum planning is 'rationalist', that is that knowledge is certain, factual and objective rather than contentious and subject to change and interpretation. This rationalist view of knowledge stems from European culture at the end of the eighteenth century, the period of the 'Enlightenment', when the aim was to formulate general laws based on observation and experiment. He argues that this stress on certainty and the one 'right' answer leads to authoritarianism. This is because if knowledge is absolute and unchanging then there cannot be legitimate alternatives to it. There is little point in discussion and dialogue as the role of the teacher is to impart a factual body of knowledge to immature recipients. This means a stress on the transmission of cognitive knowledge, subject content and values as though they were facts over education about values, skills, feelings and relationships. It also means an emphasis on teacher-centred learning over enquiry, discussion and critical analysis.

Thus through both organisation and curriculum content schooling became one of the new institutions of social control, along with prisons, hospitals and factories, that used continual surveillance to, in the words of Foucault, 'discipline and punish' in order to avoid social fragmentation and to create order and docility,

> Is it surprising that the cellular prison, with its regular chronologies, forced labour, its authorities of surveillance and registration, its experts in normality, who continue and multiply the functions of the judge, should have become the modern instrument of penality? Is it surprising

that prisons resemble factories, schools, barracks, hospitals, which all resemble prisons.

(Foucault 1977: 227–228)

The origins of mass formal schooling in Europe and America were therefore centrally concerned with social control. Schooling also played an important part in Japanese modernisation in the late nineteenth and early twentieth century with social control and indoctrination being key functions of schools where competition was intense and discipline harsh (Shipman 1971: Ch. 9).

If the origins of modern, mass schooling were concerned with social and political control, they were also reproductive and about ensuring the maintenance of the status quo. Or, as Shipman argues, 'Education not only prepares for new ways of living it also stresses attitudes to authority that help to preserve the existing distribution of power' (1971: 47). However, schooling not only played a part in reproducing existing features of society, including key forms of inequality, but actually strengthened, refined and developed such features. Simon, for example, argues that the function of the gradual provision of mass schooling in mid-nineteenth century England 'was not so much that of ensuring the reproduction of society with a divided social structure as the actual reinforcement and more precise refinement of an hierarchical society in which each stratum knew, was educated for, and accepted, its place in society' (Simon 1994: 28).

This authoritarian model of schooling with its origins in state formation, modernisation and social and political control gradually extended globally from European societies and Japan through colonisation where the key purpose of schooling was to help to control indigenous populations for the benefit of the colonial power. By the 1930s colonialism had exercised its sway over 84.6 per cent of the land surface of the globe (Loomba 1998: 15). When formal education was eventually provided missionary schools and those of the colonial state were used to control local populations by teaching the superiority of the culture of the colonising power and by supplying the subordinate personnel necessary for the effective functioning of the colonial administration (Altbach and Kelly 1978). Even if it was not always entirely successful in this, and indeed in the end helped to sow the seeds of its own destruction, the organisational style of schooling bequeathed by both the needs of industrialised mass production and then colonialism remains as a firm legacy in many post-colonial societies. Moreover, this, authoritarian, style, even if not spread directly through colonisation, was adopted and imitated by other nation states as *the* only 'modern' mass model of education.

In a study of the ex-British colony of Trinidad and Tobago, for example, the author argues that,

Schooling was intended to inculcate into the colonised a worldview of voluntary subservience to the ruling groups, and a willingness to continue to occupy positions on the lowest rungs of the occupational and social ladder. A number of effective strategies were used in the process, but the most significant among these was the instructional programmes and teaching methodologies used in colonial schools . . . Values, attitudes and behaviour were highlighted such as the habits of obedience, order, punctuality and honesty.

(London 2002: 57)

Some of the characteristics of colonial schooling in Trinidad and Tobago outlined by London include mindlessness, verbatim repetition, character development, mastery of rules as a prerequisite for application, use of abstract illustrations, monotonous drill, inculcation of specified norms for cleanliness and neatness and harsh discipline. He concludes by arguing that schooling is one of the places where colonial forms and practices have persisted and remained essentially the same throughout the post-colonial period.

A similar authoritarian stress on conformity and obedience existed, for example, in British India (Alexander 2000: 92), Francophone Africa (Moumouni 1968) and Portuguese Mozambique (Barnes 1982; Searle 1981; Azevedo 1980). In a study of contemporary schooling in India, Mali, Lebanon, Liberia, Mozambique, Pakistan, Mongolia, Ethiopia and Peru for DfID/Save the Children the authors note that,

> Almost all the systems were essentially modelled on those of the colonial powers (Britain, France, Portugal and Spain) and still use styles of classroom discipline and teaching methodology that were current a hundred years ago or more in the colonial country but have long since been repudiated there. They remain entrenched in the ex-colonies and education ministry officials continue to be resistant to the suggestion of changes that appear to offer anything less rigidly defined than their conception of the education systems of the wealthier west.
>
> (Molteno *et al.* 2000: 13)

The present writer would take issue with the extent to which in essence dominant practices in the ex-colonial powers have subsequently changed in terms of who weelds real power and control in schools as in the vast majority of instances 'it is the school that decides, the school that allows, lets, gives permission, waives, makes exceptions. It is the students who petition, request and plead' (Purpel 1989: 48). Nevertheless, the impact of colonialism on the contemporary education systems of Africa, Asia and the Caribbean is undeniable and is authoritarian in nature.

Subsequently, in Africa, many post-colonial governments did not hesitate to use schooling for political control purposes of their own (Harber 1989) while in Indonesia, 'the development of mass education at the start of the 1960s was motivated by a concern to promulgate an authoritarian political ideology and to instil an unquestioning acceptance of authority' (Watkins 1999: 4). Post-colonial governments in Malaysia have used schooling for political and ethnic control (Watson 1982) and currently in India the Hindu Nationalist government is changing the curriculum and school textbooks to reflect their ideology (Behal 2002a). In the industrialised countries the same process of using schooling for political control continues. Schooling is being used to promote right-wing Christian agendas in America (Apple 2001). In Japan the government is set to make nationalism and patriotism a compulsory part of the curriculum, which the Director of the Hiroshima Teachers' Union described as a strategy for grooming scrupulous and obedient citizens to provide a stable workforce (Fitzpatrick 2002). In Italy in 2000 the National Alliance, a member of the centre-right coalition, proposed re-writing school textbooks to remove alleged Marxist bias as the textbooks treated Mussolini's war record unfairly (Carroll 2000).

Schooling as control and surveillance

> But to go to school in a summer morn,
> O, it drives all joy away!
> *Under a cruel eye outworn*
> The little ones spend the day
> In sighing and dismay.
>   (William Blake, *The School Boy*)

In reflecting on his detailed empirical five-nation study of culture and pedagogy, Alexander (2000) was struck by the pervasive sense of control in all five schooling systems – America, England, France, India and Russia. The mechanisms, he argues, are universal – structure, curriculum, assessment, inspection, qualifications, school organisation and teaching. The controlling function is exercised at different levels,

> At national level (or state level in the United States) governments devise policies and structures, allocate budgets, determine goals, define curricula and institute mechanisms for assessing and policing what goes on at the system's lower levels. At regional and local levels such systems may be replicated or, depending on the balance of control over what goes on in the classrooms, they may simply be implemented. At school level, heads exercise varying degrees of influence or direct control over what goes on in classrooms; and at the end of the line, in classrooms, children are every day subjected to the pedagogic controls of teaching and curriculum. These controls extend into the furthest recesses of task, activity and interaction, and are mediated through routine, rule and ritual. Comparative macro–micro analysis illuminates the way these stack up and cumulatively impact on the child.
>   (Alexander 2000: 562)

A useful theoretical framework for understanding schools as systems of control that help to maintain existing power relationships was provided by Michel Foucault (1977). Foucault questioned whether historical development was taking a linear path towards rationality, enlightenment and progress. He believed that, on the contrary, modern society had developed into a more limiting and inherently 'violent' form of rationality. He argued that the regulatory practices of contemporary institutions – including schools – are even more oppressive because they are more subtle and hidden. Schools, as other forms of modern institution, control through their bureaucratic, routinised authoritarianism – constantly measuring, categorising, ordering and regulating so that control becomes accepted by the majority as normal and natural. The desired result is increased docility and obedience. This is the bells, timetables, rules, hierarchies and punishments referred to by Shipman above and witnessed in most schools internationally today.

An important aspect of this is surveillance. Foucault argued that from the eighteenth century onwards the physical design of social institutions such as working class housing estates, hospitals, asylums, prisons and schools were based on the model of the military camp where behaviour could be constantly observed and thus regulated and controlled. Foucault uses Jeremy Bentham's design of the ideal prison – the Panoptican – to describe how modern institutions survey behaviour. Like prisons, schools are divided into cells (classrooms) where the inmates are constantly watched. When people know they are being watched and will be punished for contravention of any rules then it makes it easier to control and supervise them. He argued, at a time that pre-dated the even increased contemporary emphasis on measurement and testing discussed in Chapter 8, that surveillance makes it possible 'to map aptitudes, to assess characters, to draw up rigorous classifications and, in relation to normal development, to distinguish "laziness and stubbornness" from "incurable imbecility"' (1977: 203).

We saw in Chapter 2 some of the high-tech surveillance methods that are being used in some countries to combat truancy but surveillance doesn't stop at getting pupils past the school gate. The following examples are all from England. A school in Leeds wants to build a fish tank into a glass wall for the boys and girls lavatories so that staff can see into the washrooms and keep an eye on pupils hanging around outside the cubicles. It is interesting to note that the article in the weekly *Times Educational Supplement* which described this serious proposal made absolutely no mention of human rights issues (Williams 2001). Schools in England are also introducing expensive electronic swipe card systems to keep a constant all day check on pupils' attendance at school and at individual lessons. One school in Manchester had reduced truancy from 400 a day to 50 a day, though the headteacher did also admit that it was also important to try to make school more interesting so that pupils would want to stay (Revell 2002). Human rights groups have criticised schools for taking electronic fingerprints of pupils instead of issuing library cards. As many as 200,000 primary and secondary pupils have been fingerprinted in 350 schools, according to Privacy International, which has called for the removal of high-tech scanning equipment (*Times Educational Supplement* 26/7/2002). A prototype of a system of radar wrist and ankle tags is also being developed to help teachers keep track of pupils on class trips or to stop them leaving the school grounds. Each pupil is tagged and teachers have a pager-style device which tells them how far away they are. The civil rights group Liberty said that it feared that they could become a part of everyday life in the school classroom. Schools can take part in online consultation on the devices and enter a prize draw to win £500 by visiting the website (Shaw 2003).

It may be that this apparatus of control and surveillance aimed at docility does not work on all pupils and many rebel, disobey and react violently. Also, schooling as a means of social control is only inefficiently administered in many developing countries – what elsewhere we termed 'bureaucratic facades' and 'messy authoritarianism' (Harber and Davies 1997: Ch. 3). Also, as noted in Chapter 3, in some of the schools in New York teacher surveillance has given way to surveillance by metal detectors and security guards (Devine 1996). However, for present purposes it is the *attempt* to control and the resulting authoritarian school structures that are important in understanding how schools can be, and regularly are, sites of violence towards pupils. It is also very important to stress that this external authoritarian control is not the same as democratic control with its emphasis on internal *group* and *self* regulation, discipline and control.

A final point in relation to schooling for control is the seeming paradox that schools in many countries with democratic political institutions educate for control via authoritarian school structures and curricula as do schools under authoritarian political regimes. How does democracy survive in such circumstances? First, it has to be said that there are often differences of degree if not of kind. Forms of control in and of schools in authoritarian political systems may be more explicit and harsh than in democracies. However, as argued in Chapter 2 and in this chapter, schools operating in democratic political systems nevertheless socialise towards authoritarian values in the lack of real power and participation afforded to learners. The main argument is that schools in democracies are not doing enough either to support democracy or, in particular, to deepen and strengthen it. Democracy can be created and learned and it can be lost and forgotten – and there are many historical examples going both ways. If schooling does not consciously try to contribute to the development of a democratic political culture supportive of democratic political institutions – the political knowledge, skills, values and behaviour of a population – then democracy is always fragile and at risk. This, for example, was the argument behind the government initiated Crick Report on Education for Democratic Citizenship in England, one of the oldest democracies in the world, which recommended that education for democratic citizenship be introduced as a key part of the curriculum. The report expressed genuine concern at levels of political alienation, apathy and cynicism among the population and the risk that this posed to democracy (Advisory Group on Citizenship 1998).

Carr and Hartnett (1996: Ch. 2) also make a useful distinction between what they term 'classical' democracy which had its origins in ancient Greece, and 'contemporary' forms of democracy. They argue that in modern times the former has been rejected as utopian. Studies of the actual workings of democracies in mass industrialised societies suggest that, rather than a more participant understanding of 'rule by the people', what occurs in practice is more minimal. People have a right to choose between rival political élites at regular elections much as consumers choose between products in the market place. The role of citizens is therefore more limited than in classical democracy and high levels of passivity and political apathy are actually important to maintain stability and guard against system overload.

A core principle of classical democracy is that individuals are able to participate in the life of their society, including decision making. In such a society citizens enjoy equal opportunities for self-development, self-fulfilment and self-determination. This requires a society in which there is a knowledgeable and informed citizenry capable of participating in democratic political debate on equal terms. A core principle of contemporary democracy, on the other hand, is that it provides a means of selecting political leaders which curtails an excess or abuse of power through certain empirical conditions including regular elections, universal suffrage, rival political parties, a representative system of government, a free press and an independent judiciary. It is assumed that people have no obligation to participate in decision making and most ordinary people have no desire to do so. A rigid distinction is therefore made between an active élite political leadership and the passive majority of ordinary citizens. Democracy flourishes, according to this model, in an individualistic society with a competitive market economy and with minimal state intervention. This does not require conscious or explicit education for democracy as active citizens are not desirable.

Much of schooling in liberal democracies would provide support for this contemporary model of democracy or an even more limited version of it. A crucial difference between the two models, however, is the commitment to develop a democratic *society* as well as political system. Fuller versions of democracy require much greater levels of democracy and equality in our daily interactions, relationships and behaviours in the workplace and in social and domestic activities. This requires a conscious attempt to remove prejudice and discrimination on the basis of, for example, race, class, gender, sexual orientation, religion, disability and age. It is here that the authoritarian model of schooling with its emphasis on cognitive knowledge and a narrow range of skills and its general reluctance to engage with controversial issues, critical social and political analysis, feelings, identities and relationships is particularly supportive of a non-democratic society under both authoritarian and democratic political systems.

Schooling as reproduction and perpetration

It is widely thought that education in the shape of formal schooling can change society for the better and indeed it has this potential. Through meritocratic education, the argument goes, greater productivity, prosperity and equality can be achieved. Theoretical discussions of education and social change often stress the beneficial role of schooling, for example human capital theory in relation to greater individual and social economic productivity and modernisation theory in terms of the adoption of social values that enhance the quality of life (Fagerlind and Saha 1989: Chs 1–4). While it will be argued in the final chapter that even these are only inherently and truly beneficial in the framework of an education firmly aimed at democracy, human rights and peace, the purpose of the present section is to suggest that schooling also has two other significant roles. The first is reproduction. This is where schooling does not act as an agent of change but simply reproduces characteristics of the surrounding society. One example of this is the neo-Marxist analysis of the role of schooling in reproducing rather than ameliorating social class inequalities in society through reproducing the social relations of work, inequality and exploitation in the school and classroom (Bowles and Gintis 1976; Levin 1987; Meighan 1997: Ch. 26). Working-class children go to school, experience the social relationships and expectations that correspond to working-class employment and then leave school to go into working-class jobs – and their prospects are even worse if they rebel (Willis 1977). If control is a, if not the, major function of schooling then it must play a significant part in reproducing what already is and therefore supporting the status quo. The situation of most working-class children is not actively harmed according to this analysis, it is just that, despite the rhetorical claims of equal opportunity surrounding formal education, their life chances are not actually improved. Similarly, we have argued elsewhere that schools in developing countries often do not act as the unproblematic agents of social modernisation but that in 'prismatic' societies schools are as likely to reflect and reproduce the characteristics and practices of the surrounding culture and economic system as to fundamentally change them (Harber and Davies 1997: Ch. 6).

In terms of the role of schooling in relation to violence, the forms of violence by omission discussed in Chapter 3 could be seen as essentially reproductive. By doing nothing or ignoring a negative or dangerous aspect of the surrounding society – bullying, infection by HIV/AIDS, racism, gendered sexual violence and violence itself – the role of schools can be said to be reproductive. However, all too often, given that schooling is supposed to be an enlightened and beneficial institution, schooling isn't only reproductive. In terms of schooling as a violent institution we need to go beyond schooling as reproduction to look at schooling as *perpetration*. This is because schooling not only reproduces some significant forms of violence that exist in the wider society, it actively perpetrates them thereby adding to the problem, making it worse and multiplying it. Indeed, in relation to schooling it is possible to borrow from economics and talk of a 'multiplier effect' in relation to violence.

In studying schools as organisations Handy (1984) used a survey in which he asked teachers in schools in England 'how many people are there in this organisation?'. They answered 10 or 70 or whatever the number of teachers – they nearly always left out the pupils as human beings. This would be an interesting question to ask teachers and educational adminis-trators worldwide. The role of schooling in perpetrating and multiplying violence can only be understood in terms of its dehumanising nature. Established as authoritarian bureaucracies for the purposes of control, schools, especially large ones, find it very difficult to see the individual's or even the group's needs and peculiarities and indeed they are not necessarily designed to do so. They deny fundamental human rights of participation, voice and consent to pupils – and often teachers as well who follow orders from above.

How does schooling dehumanise and therefore perpetrate and multiply violence according to the five dimensions of violence discussed in the remaining chapters of this book?

Corporal punishment

Physical violence against children in the form of corporal punishment is still widespread in schools globally as Chapter 5 demonstrates. This stems from the need to reinforce order and control in an authoritarian context but it is also important that in such a context children are not seen as fully human. Justifications for the use of corporal punishment in terms of the immaturity of young people suggest that simply being young denies the existence of the human right not to be subject to cruel and degrading punishment. The idea and practice of the physical punishment of young people may exist in the wider society but its use in schools has a multiplier effect because it both legitimates violence by the stronger against the weaker and increases the chance of the child him- or herself becoming more violent and therefore adds to the level of violence in society as a whole.

Racism

School authoritarianism is also associated with racism. In a setting which stresses cognitive knowledge and where controversial issues and alternative viewpoints tend not to be discussed then not only can racist views go unchallenged but the system itself can actively perpetrate racist values.

If an education system stresses control and obedience and at the same time actively paints a picture of an enemy 'other' as evil or inhuman this dehumanises both sides and significantly contributes to levels of violence between groups and communities. Chapter 6 discusses instances of schools actively promoting racism.

Gender

Schools that ignore sexism in the wider society or between pupils are helping to reproduce it, including physically violent forms of sexism such as harassment and rape. However, schools in some societies are more directly and actively involved in perpetrating gender violence through the actions of male teachers and the messages transmitted by schooling. The authoritarianism of the school stresses obedience and that one's elders should not be questioned, particularly if they are male. This makes it more difficult for female students in these contexts to question and resist unwanted sexual demands or to seek justice if sex is physically enforced. In some countries this brings with it a serious risk of infection with HIV/AIDS. Moreover, schools are also involved in the perpetration of hegemonic forms of masculine culture that regard females as unequal and therefore less human and which justify and multiply not only sexual violence but violence in general. Chapter 7 discusses ways in which schools help to perpetrate sexual violence against females and masculine forms of violent identity in general.

Stress, anxiety and testing

Control through regulation, standardisation, classification and surveillance involves regular measurement and ranking through testing, examinations and other forms of assessment. Schools themselves are increasingly judged, inspected and ranked in the process. One key purpose of testing in terms of economic control is screening and selection so as to both pass and to fail enough learners to maintain the scarcity and hence value of both higher level qualifications and types of occupation in the labour market. A second is to politically control schools through accountability mechanisms which includes evaluating the success or failure of their pupils in examinations. Schools are now increasingly more competitive and test-driven than any other branch of society. Pupils (and teachers) are treated not as individual human beings with multiple dimensions to their lives and learning but as commodities in a production process that can be subject to 'quality control' through testing. Hence the rarity of genuine diagnostic testing of pupils. Such testing comes at a price for pupils who can suffer considerable stress and anxiety resulting in mental and physical harm.

Militarisation

Historically there has been a relationship between schools and the military. In some ways the organisation of schooling – authoritarianism, control, obedience and regimentation – mirrors or corresponds to military organisation. Internationally, armies are not primarily noted for their humanity and indeed are not created for this purpose, even though they are occasionally involved in humanitarian roles. Some societies and some schools have actively taught military values and provided military training, including the handling of weaponry and the consideration of military tactics. This is often done to defend or promote a country or a particular ideology. In encouraging an arms-based military mentality among people who will not necessarily go on to become highly trained professional and disciplined soldiers, schooling is actively contributing to the multiplication of people able and willing to use violent weaponry in society. The militarisation of schooling will be discussed in Chapter 9.

Conclusion

Historically, a key purpose for the creation of mass systems of formal schooling in industrialising countries was control and surveillance and preparation for subordinate roles in the workplace and wider society. This is why schooling was based on authoritarian modes of organisation. This model was spread by the need to control populations in the colonies. The model in its fundamentals has proved remarkably impervious to change, despite considerable change in both the workplace and surrounding societies. While its 'modern', bureaucratic form may well be responsible for change in relation to economic productivity and social modernisation, schooling also reproduces key negative aspects of the surrounding society such as inequalities based on race, class and gender. However, its authoritarian nature also allows it to go further than this and to actively increase or multiply negative aspects as well, including violent ones. It is therefore time to add another dimension to discussions of the role of schooling in relation to society, that of active perpetration of violence.

We need to ask what it is about schooling that makes society worse as well as what schooling does to make society better or to keep it the same. As the following chapters will demonstrate, we need to consider *inhuman* capital theory in relation to the role of schooling.

5 Schooling as terrorism
Physical punishment

> State parties shall take all appropriate legislative, administrative, social and educational measures to protect the child from all forms of physical . . . violence, injury or abuse . . . while in the care of parent(s) . . . or any other person who has the care of the child.
>
> (United Nations Convention on the Rights of the Child, 1989, Article 19)

Introduction

A true story. I was driving into work one day in May 2002 listening to a discussion on the radio. The participants were discussing servant/master relationships. One contributor from India said that he had seen a servant tied to a post and whipped. Another said she had seen a similar thing in South Africa in the last decade. A third said he had seen the same thing – only at school. All the participants burst out laughing. Why was this funny? Corporal punishment at schools is a degrading and humiliating act of violence and is a denial of the fundamental rights of the child as set out above. Yet the physical punishment of children is still commonplace, widely supported and justified as being 'for your own good'.

The World Health Organization has recently reviewed research revealing high levels of physical punishment and abuse of children within families in a diverse range of countries – USA, Egypt, South Korea, Romania, Ethiopia, Chile, India and the Philippines (2002: 62–63). This list should certainly include the UK where the government has refused to ban physical punishment in the home and no doubt other countries should be included as well. While violence towards children in the home is beyond the scope of this book, there is a connection with violence in the school. If parents themselves were beaten at school – an institution sanctioned and legitimated by the state and their own parents who sent them there – then this must have provided an influential behavioural role model. Physical punishment at school must contribute to the idea that this is a normal and acceptable form of punishment in a society and that it can be used against children both in the home and at school. In this way physical punishment at school not only affects children at school but in the home as well as it does nothing to break the cycle of violence. How and why has schooling become associated with violence in the form of physical punishment?

Schooling and physical punishment

It has been argued that the control and surveillance origins of formal schooling are reflected in its authoritarian nature. Pupils internationally tend to have very little control over what they learn, when, where and how and also very little say in how their schools are organised. A key element of these authoritarian relationships is the perceived right of teachers to punish, inherent in the need to maintain control and order. As one American writer put it,

> Systemic violence begins with the expectation that all students of similar ages should and can learn the same things. Children are placed with large groups of similarly aged students and teachers are forced to adopt methods of control and routine that would be better left to the military, the workforce or the penal system . . . In a quest for conformity, students are monitored in their coming and going, they are required to carry hall passes and must seek permission to leave the room. Their activities are directed and timed and their learning is scheduled into periods of work followed by short breaks. Such regimentation requires rules and punishment and administrative models that rely on differentiated power relations.
>
> (Ross Epp 1996: 17)

The role of punishment in reinforcing order in schools in developing countries has also been commented on in a joint publication of the British Department for International Development and Save the Children which noted that in some schools in a range of countries they studied (India, Mali, Lebanon, Liberia, Mozambique, Pakistan, Mongolia, Ethiopia and Peru),

> it is almost certainly more damaging for children to be in school than out of it. Children whose days are spent herding animals rather than sitting in a classroom at least develop skills of problem solving and independence while the supposedly luckier ones in school are stunted in their mental, physical and emotional development by being rendered passive and having to spend hours each day in a crowded room under the control of an adult who punishes them for any normal level of activity such as moving or speaking.
>
> (Molteno *et al.* 2000: 12–13)

Such control and order has consistently been associated with violent imposition,

From their inception, formal schools in Western capitalist societies have been designed to discipline bodies as well as to regulate minds. A key purpose of modern state schooling has been the formation and conduct of beliefs, as well as the acquisition of prescribed knowledge. School discipline has frequently been overt and physically violent, with students most often the target of teacher-administered punishment.

(Rousmaniere *et al.* 1997: 3)

In her study of corporal punishment and children's rights, Parker-Jenkins argues that the history of childhood, at least in Western societies, chronicles the regular abuse and terrorising of children by their caretakers and that an expectation that child-rearing and corporal punishment should go hand in hand has been carried over into school life. In Victorian Britain, at the time when a mass schooling system was developing that would influence many other parts of the globe through colonialism, the religious concept of 'original sin' justified physically beating evil out of children in schools. She adds that, apart from the contention that corporal punishment derived its legitimacy from God, there was little hesitation in using corporal punishment to enforce the two imperatives which dominated nineteenth-century discussion of the education of children – obedience and duty. She notes that,

A hallmark of 'education for the masses' was low cost and large class sizes. Within such a situation, and given the Victorian predilection for physical chastisement, it is perhaps not surprising that the disciplinary sanction was used widely.

(1999: 6)

Indeed, as Parker-Jenkins shows, in Britain law courts consistently upheld the right of schools to beat children and corporal punishment was only finally banned in state schools in 1986 as a result of legal decisions stemming from European courts in Strasbourg. However, the ban on corporal punishment was only extended to children in all schools as late as 1999.

Corporal punishment has been, and still widely is, used in schools internationally. A major factor in its global spread was colonialism, particularly British colonialism. In Africa, for example, it has been argued that although corporal punishment is now justified on the grounds that it is 'part of African culture', evidence on pre-colonial education systems suggests that this is unlikely. As Tafa argues in relation to pre-colonial Botswana, where corporal punishment is still widely used in schools, 'There is no evidence to suggest that children were flogged every step of the way' (2002: 23). He notes that when neighbouring Zambia banned caning in 2000 it was described as 'a brutal relic of British rule'. He argues that,

Caning became ingrained in the popular minds as critical to school discipline hence the common refrain that its abolition equals classroom disorder and failure. The result is a cycle of caning transmitted from one generation to another and justified on the basis of experience and sentiment . . . In a class of 35–40 authoritarianism is a means of orchestrating 'mob control'. Instant punishment and military style parades typical of Botswana schools are all about social control. Teachers are saddled with systemic constraints of large and mixed class sizes for which no extra resources were made available.

(Tafa 2002: 23)

A Human Rights Watch study of the widespread use of corporal punishment in Kenyan schools noted that 'The Kenyan school system arose in the days of the British colonial government and adopted nineteenth century British traditions of school discipline, including the widespread use of the cane' (1999a: 7–8). A similar case has been argued for its origins in Barbados (Anderson and Payne 1994). However, Portuguese colonialism also seems to have helped caning to spread. In Mozambique under Portuguese colonial control,

Teachers mercilessly beat children, insulted them, made them work in the fields, compelled them to spend hours kneeling on brick floors, pulled their ears, kicked them, and in some instances made them bleed. When one visited a Mozambican school in the 1960s, one invariably found two devices of punishment: a stick or whip and a palmatoria – a wooden device shaped like an arm and a hand. The hand part had several holes so that when it struck the child's hand it sucked some of the flesh, causing severe pain.

(Azevedo 1980: 200)

Before discussing the overwhelmingly negative consequences of the use of physical violence as punishment in schools, it is necessary to examine the evidence that corporal punishment is still a significant feature of schooling internationally.

Corporal punishment and schooling

The World Health Organization reports that corporal punishment in schools in the form of hitting, punching, beating or kicking remains legal in at least 65 countries, despite the fact that the United Nations Committee on the Rights of the Child has underlined that corporal punishment is incompatible with the Convention. It notes that 'Where the practice has not been persistently confronted by legal reform and public education, the few existing prevalence studies suggest it remains extremely common' (WHO 2002: 64). In a further range of countries where it has been officially banned, such as South Africa, it is still in use in many schools as will be seen below. This suggests that corporal punishment is regularly used in schools in between at least one-third and one-half of all countries in the world. Furthermore in others it has only been banned relatively recently and there are still many people who have been affected by the practice who are themselves now parents and teachers and who have positions of responsibility over others. In other societies where corporal punishment has finally been banned, there are still many who desire its return. A survey of 1000 parents in England and Wales in 2000, for example, found that 51 per cent thought that corporal punishment should be reintroduced in schools (Carvel 2000). In Canada a 1990 study of the perceptions of school authorities (teachers, principals, superintendents, Department of Education officials and school board trustees) regarding the rights of students and parents reported that 79 per cent said corporal punishment can be justified (cited in Ross Epp 1996: 177).

America is currently fighting a 'war on terrorism'. Terrorism can be defined as the use of violence to achieve political ends. Schooling involves the use of power and physical violence to impose political ends of control and authority so perhaps America is a good place to begin a geographical review of corporal punishment in schools. America is also one of the two countries in the world (the other being Somalia) not to have signed the UN Convention on the Rights of the Child. Ross Epp set her American higher education students an exercise whereby they were asked to recall experiences from their own schooling. Physical punishment (strappings, ear pullings, cheek pinchings, bottom slappings) were common in the responses – often in regard to minor infractions of the rules. Students reported feeling fear, humiliation, embarrassment and exclusion as a result of the punishments (Ross Epp 1996: 14–15). At the end of the 1990s corporal punishment was still widely used and approved of in America and was legal in 27 out of 50 states (Parker-Jenkins 1999: 111). Even doctors play a role in the social support of corporal punishment. In a survey in the early 1990s two out of three care physicians approved of the use of physical punishment (cited in Kohn 1993: 348–349).

In terms of South and Central America and the Caribbean, Abello (1997: 458) writes of the use of pinching, pulling ears/arms/hair, hitting with a ruler and shaking by teachers in schools in Colombia while in Mexican schools Martin (1994: 167) talks of 'the pervasiveness of pupil preoccupation with teacher heavy-handedness' with typical comments from pupils referring to teachers beating pupils. Indeed, between a fifth and a quarter of pupils interviewed said that this contributed to pupil drop out (push out). One conclusion that Martin reaches is that 'basic enthusiasm for studying is turned to a distaste for it because of the bullying by teachers of their pupils' and he uses a quote from an American primary pupil in what he describes as one of the 'most renowned and unpretentiously incisive books on primary education': 'You know, kids really like to learn; we just don't like being pushed around' (Holt 1969: 170). A survey of children at infant, junior and secondary schools in Barbados found that 95 per cent of boys and 92 per cent of girls had experienced being caned/flogged at school and that there was widespread support for this even though a few questions were starting to be asked (Anderson and Payneand 1994: 383–384).

In India one education correspondent noted that 'Much teaching is conducted in an abusive and callous manner. For these children, school does not open up a new world of knowledge and learning. . . . The most ubiquitous teaching aid is the stick' (Bates 2000a). In 1998 parents called for a ban on corporal punishment in schools after a 13-year-old in Delhi lost an eye when a teacher threw a blackboard duster at him. A few months before a teacher bit off a student's ear to punish him for a prank. Many schoolchildren said they had nightmares about going to school, especially if they had not finished their homework. Inquiries showed that teachers routinely slap students (Surnoor and Behal 1998). In 2002 Karnataka State in southern India said that it was going to crack down on corporal punishment after a 10-year-old girl died at school. The pupil was ordered to run three times around the school and twice up and down the stairs after turning up late for a PE class. The autopsy report suggested that the girl had been punished soon after lunch and could have died choking on the food she regurgitated due to physical stress (Behal 2002b). One researcher found common and regular use of birching in three different types of nursery and primary school in India – usually involving striking the child's bare thigh, often in response to the child making a mistake. This practice was supported by parents (Nieuwenhuys 1994: 54–55).

One writer comparing the practice of schooling in Japan to the tenets of the UN Convention on the Rights of the Child noted that there is a rule prohibiting corporal punishment dating from 1947,

> However, the number of teachers ready to use corporal punishment on children in contradiction of this rule has been increasing. According to a survey conducted by the Ministry of Education, it is known that 599 teachers used corporal punishment in 1996. In the same year 2005 children were victims of corporal punishment at school. These figures fail to represent the full extent of the problem. However, the number of teachers losing their jobs due to illegal use of corporal punishment is almost none.
>
> (Kawaguchi 2000: 501)

In South Korea corporal punishment is still common practice in schools and is not seen as an educational problem, despite being illegal. Teachers still hit students with a ruler or stick, kick them and verbally abuse them and pupils have no means of appeal. The worst case on record is that of a 12-year-old boy who died after being beaten by teachers in 1993. Indeed, it is seen as an act of 'love' and supposedly builds character and prepares students for the real world (Kang 2002: 321–322). In Thailand caning was only finally outlawed at the end of 2000 – where it was used in colleges and universities as well as schools. The change was part of a wider reform to try to introduce more student-centred methods. In 2000 several children had been badly beaten by teachers, one about the head with a guitar. Teachers accused of beating their pupils too harshly typically pressured parents to withdraw their complaints or, in serious cases, ended up being transferred by their superiors to other schools rather than face criminal action (West 2000).

Corporal punishment also exists in some countries in the schools of North Africa and the Middle East. Salmi (1999: 9–10) notes that in Morocco 'most primary teachers work with a ruler, a stick or a piece of rubber garden hose which are generously used to hit the children'. In Palestine corporal punishment is widely used in schools, often, as elsewhere, accompanied by verbal violence – scornful expressions, humiliating words and pejorative judgements (Mansour 1996: 306). A survey of 1170 students attending Bedouin schools in Israel found that 68 per cent of the children reported witnessing some physical abuse by teachers in the classroom and 95 per cent witnessed at least some psychological or physical punishment. The most frequent physical abuse mentioned by students was slapping, kicking, twisting ears or grabbing or pushing. This was despite a rule of the Israeli Ministry of Education which prohibits such practices (Elbedour *et al.* 1997).

Corporal punishment is also commonplace in many African schools. A lengthy and detailed study of Kenyan schools, for example, summarised its findings thus,

> For most Kenyan children, violence is a regular part of the school experience. Teachers use caning, slapping and whipping to maintain classroom discipline and to punish children for poor academic performance. The infliction of corporal punishment is routine, arbitrary and often brutal. Bruises and cuts are regular by-products of school punishments and more severe injuries (broken bones, knocked-out teeth, internal bleeding) are not infrequent. At times, beatings by teachers leave children permanently disfigured, disabled or dead.
>
> (Human Rights Watch 1999a: 3)

This is despite the case that, although legal at that time, there were supposed to be strict rules about the use of corporal punishment in Kenyan schools. The government of Kenya banned corporal punishment at the end of 2001 in a bid to end unrest in schools but it seems very unlikely that the practice will disappear overnight. Indeed, it was reported that many heads and high ranking officials were demanding a return of corporal punishment *because* of unrest in schools (Kigotho 2001). More surprisingly, it was reported that staff in several schools have been caned in front of pupils by union officials for continuing to teach despite a national strike (Kigotho 2002).

A survey of 261 teachers in The Gambia showed that 92 per cent had caned a child and that the use of corporal punishment was not carried out in accordance with government regulations (Sey 2000: 218). Corporal punishment was reported to be widespread in South Kivu Province of the Democratic Republic of the Congo (Balegamire 1999) and in Ghana (Hedges 2002: 132). A study of the socialisation of new teachers in Botswana described the routinisation of birching in schools. The fieldnotes of the research refer to the ubiquitous canes, beatings witnessed, teachers using canes as teaching aids and graphic teachers' stories about caning. Again, there are strict rules about the use of corporal punishment in schools in Botswana but these are honoured more in the breach than in the observance. Caning was administered by all and sundry – student teachers, untrained teachers, pupils themselves, porters and night-watchmen. The pupils themselves seemed to condone this widespread and regular use of corporal punishment (Tafa 2002).

A study in South Africa sheds some light on this latter point. Corporal punishment is now illegal in South Africa but a survey of 750 school pupils in KwaZulu Natal found that it is still commonly used and supported by parents and pupils. Among African pupils from township schools there was particularly strong public endorsement of corporal punishment. However, at the same time, the majority of the very same pupils whose public discourse supported corporal punishment said that they felt anger, hurt and sadness as a result of corporal punishment and, almost the opposite, positive feelings about consultative mechanisms of discipline in relation to discussing problems with the teacher in class (Morrell 1999). What seemed to be happening was that pupils were denying their own private knowledge of the experience of corporal punishment as it contradicted the more powerful and widely accepted public discourse in favour of corporal punishment.

The impact of violent punishment in schools

> The twentieth century will be remembered as a century marked by violence. It burdens us with its legacy of mass destruction, of violence inflicted on a scale never seen and never possible before in human history. Less visible, but even more widespread, is the legacy of day-to-day individual suffering. It is the pain of children who are abused by people who should protect them. . . . This suffering is a legacy that reproduces itself, as new generations learn from the violence of generations past, as victims learn from victimisers . . . *Violence thrives in the absence of democracy, respect for human rights and good governance.*
> (Nelson Mandela, quoted in WHO 2002: ix, author's italics)

> My pedagogy is hard . . . I want the young to be violent, domineering, undismayed, cruel. They must be able to bear pain. There must be nothing gentle or weak about them.
> (Adolf Hitler quoted in Miller 1987: 142)

There is strong and consistent research evidence that physical punishment and the deliberate humiliation of children is significantly linked with the development of violent attitudes and actions in later life. However, as the Gulbenkian Commission on Children and Violence notes, this knowledge seems to be 'counter-intuitive', hence the enduring support for corporal punishment among teachers, parents and pupils internationally (Gulbenkian Foundation 1995: 47).

South Africa made corporal punishment in schools illegal in 1997, though as we have seen it is still commonly used. In 2000 the South African Department of Education published a document entitled *Guidelines for Alternatives to Corporal Punishment*. This provides a very useful and concise summary not only of alternatives to corporal punishment but of some of the main reasons why the results of corporal punishment in schools internationally are comprehensively negative. It is worth repeating here in full:

> Extensive research shows that corporal punishment does not achieve the desired end – a culture of learning and discipline in the classroom. Instead violence begets violence. Children exposed to violence in their homes and at school tend to use violence to solve problems, both as children and as adults. Key research findings show that corporal punishment,
>
> - Does not build a culture of human rights, tolerance and respect
> - Does not stop bad behaviour of difficult children. Instead, these children are punished over and over again for the same offences
> - Does not nurture self-discipline in children. Instead, it provokes aggression and feelings of revenge and leads to anti-social behaviour
> - Does not make children feel responsible for their own actions. They worry about being caught, not about personal responsibilities. This undermines the growth of self-discipline in children
> - Takes children's focus away from the wrongdoing to the act of beating itself. Some learners brag about being beaten as something to be proud of, as a badge of bravery or success
> - Undermines a caring relationship between learner and educator, which is critical for the development of all learners, particularly those with behavioural difficulties
> - Stands in the way of proper communication between the educator and the learner and therefore hides the real problems behind misconduct which need to be tackled, such as trauma, poverty-related problems and conflict at home
> - Is an excuse for educators not to find more constructive approaches to discipline in the classroom and therefore reinforces bad or lazy teaching practices
> - Has been shown to contribute to truancy and drop-out rates in South African schools

- Is usually used by educators in a prejudiced way. Those learners who are usually beaten tend to be older than their peers, from poor homes, black rather than white, boys rather than girls
- Helps accelerate difficult or rebellious learners down a path of violence and gangsterism.

(South African Department of Education 2000: 7–8)

One negative consequence not mentioned is the impact it has on the health of the child. In the immediate term this can be pain, bleeding and broken limbs as well as psychological pain in the form of humiliation. However, there can be longer term consequences as well. The World Health Organization, which explicitly includes corporal punishment in school as part of child abuse, states that,

> Importantly there is now evidence that major adult forms of illness – including ischaemic heart disease, cancer, chronic lung disease, irritable bowl syndrome and fibromyalgia – are related to experiences of abuse during childhood. The apparent mechanism to explain these results is the adoption of behavioural risk factors such as smoking, alcohol abuse, poor diet and lack of exercise. . . . Similarly there are many studies demonstrating short-term and long-term psychological damage. Some children have a few symptoms that do not reach clinical levels of concern, or else are at clinical levels but not as high as in children generally seen in clinical settings. Other survivors have serious psychiatric symptoms, such as depression, anxiety, substance abuse, aggression, shame or cognitive impairments. Finally, some children meet the full criteria for psychiatric illnesses that include post-traumatic stress disorder, major depression, anxiety disorders and sleep disorders.
>
> (WHO 2002: 69–70)

Human Rights Watch, reviewing research on the psychological effects of corporal punishment in schools, stated that possible results include depression, withdrawal, anxiety, tension and in older children substance abuse, interference with school work and precocious sexual behaviour. These psychological conditions arise out of children's inability to cope with the humiliation and degradation that they experience. There is no socially acceptable manner for them to express their feelings and if they act out their frustrations they will be further punished. At home they may find little consolation or support if parents support teachers' actions. The forbidden and repressed anger can be manifested as hatred towards self and others (Human Rights Watch 1999a: 45–46). The final section of this chapter therefore focuses on the role of corporal punishment in schools in helping to reproduce and perpetuate violence in society.

Violence reproduces violence

The psychoanalyst Alice Miller wrote,

> When people who have been beaten or spanked as children attempt to play down the consequences by setting themselves up as examples, even claiming it was good for them, they are inevitably contributing to the continuation of cruelty in the world by this refusal to take their childhood tragedies seriously. Taking over this attitude, their children, pupils, and students will in turn beat their own children, citing their parents, teachers and professors as authorities.
>
> (1987: xii)

The Gulbenkian Report on children and violence had a section 'Discipline and Punishment'. In this it studied international reviews of research evidence on the impact of violent forms of physical punishment. The American Psychological Association said that physical punishment increased the probability of aggressive and violent behaviour. The Australian National Committee on Violence concluded that the child may well observe and copy aggressive actions. A longitudinal study over three generations in New York state found that a violent upbringing contributed to becoming violent adults and a study in America that was replicated in Finland, Poland, Holland, Australia and Israel found that physical punishment by parents contributed significantly to aggression in both boys and girls. Similar research findings from the UK are also reviewed (Gulbenkian Foundation 1995: 50–52). It concludes the section by quoting from a detailed study by Strauss,

> Research over the past 40 years has been remarkably consistent in showing that hitting children increases the chances of a child becoming physically aggressive, delinquent or both. The research in this book shows that corporal punishment leaves invisible scars that affect many aspects of life.
>
> (1994: 186)

In the review of research which accompanies their study of abusive behaviour in Bedouin schools in Israel, Elbedour and colleagues note that 'a victim of abuse will often treat others abusively, increasing the likelihood that the destruction will continue exponentially' and that 'Children learn to imitate violent behaviour and value it as a coping mechanism for survival, whether for self-defence or status-seeking' (1997: 202). Similarly, Kohn reviews research evidence from America that supports his contention that,

> Regardless of what we are trying to get across by spanking, paddling or slapping them, the messages that actually come through are these: 'violence is an acceptable way of expressing anger' and 'If you are

powerful enough you can get away with hurting someone'. For decades, researchers have consistently found that children subjected to physical punishment tend to be more aggressive than their peers, and will likely grow up to use violence on their own children. These effects are not confined to victims of what is legally classified as abuse: even 'acceptable' levels of physical punishment may perpetuate aggression and unhappiness.

(1993: 167)

The Human Rights Watch study of corporal punishment in Kenya reviewed similar international evidence but also found evidence from Kenya that violence by the school helps to breed violence. One headteacher of a school said 'one thing leads to another; show me a school that has excessive corporal punishment and I'll show you a school that has bullying'. The chairperson of the Alliance for the Advancement of the Rights of the Child in Kenya said that when children act out what takes place in school, the child 'teacher' beats the 'pupils'. She added 'They are socialised to think that (hitting) is what the teacher does'. The Kenyan children interviewed affirmed that they perceived corporal punishment as humiliating, painful, frightening and anger-inspiring (Human Rights Watch 1999a: 46–47).

While violence is present in some form in many societies, Palestine has been one of the societies most associated with violence internationally now for some years. While macro political forces are behind the violence, the school is not irrelevant and corporal punishment plays a part in adding to the atmosphere of violence,

> The school reproduces on a smaller scale the dynamic forces which move society: it has also suffered the adverse effects of occupation and continues to suffer from limited budgets. As a result, it imposes intense institutional violence both on teachers and on pupils. The teachers are subjected to particularly stressful working conditions (overcrowded classrooms, lack of training, no in-service training, very low salaries, no promotion prospects and so on) and many pupils pile up a history of failure, humiliation and frustration in the school system. We have a favourable breeding ground for violent behaviour, in the absence of prospects for various actors. It is a fact that corporal punishment is widely used, and despite the lack of reliable data there are signs that a degree of insecurity governs relations between pupils themselves and between pupils and their teachers.

(Mansour 1996: 308–309)

Conclusion

In relation to physical punishment, schools in many countries are involved in both the perpetration of violence and the perpetuation of violence.

Schools that practice this violence certainly don't make society a better place and don't just reproduce violence – they actively help to produce it. Meanwhile children are harmed by these violent practices. There may be no obligation on America or Somalia to cease this form of terrorism as they are not signatories of the UN Convention on the Rights of the Child but all other states should ban its use immediately.

6 Schooling and learning to hate the 'other'

Finally, there is the moulding of the perpetrators, the archetypal 'loyal subjects', without whose blind obedience, deference to authority and excessive trust in authority no genocide could ever take place.

(Scherrer 2002: 119 on the Rwandan genocide of 1994)

We, as adults, must acknowledge that we routinely abuse our power over children. A visiting Martian would have great difficulty in accepting that we are committed to children's education, seeing that in one country we are expelling girls from school if they wear a headscarf, while in another we are expelling them from school unless they wear a headscarf! Sadly, nobody would be able to persuade the visiting Martian that we really care about education.

(Katarina Tomaoevski, Special Rapporteur to the UN Commission on Human Rights, *Independent* 10/9/99)

Introduction

In discussing plural societies words like 'race', 'ethnicity', 'tribe' and 'nation' are frequently used for groups described as having some physical or cultural features in common. However, there is no universal use and meaning given to such words as each is socially and politically constructed and reconstructed in a particular regional, national or local context. The social construction of the characteristics of 'we' and 'they' identities – who is included and who is excluded – and the linguistic labels attached vary globally. Similarly the nature of the prejudice, hostility and unequal treatment that occurs based on one group's attitudes of difference and/or superiority/inferiority varies both geographically and over time. This is why it is easier to talk in general terms about the 'other' as identified and defined by the groups operating in a particular context at a particular moment (Troyna 1993: 12–15).

Schooling has always played a part, via socialisation and indoctrination, in the creation, reproduction and modification of such group identities and stereotypes. Colonial education, for example, played a major role in this and has left a legacy of classifications, labels and negative relationships that still influence the politics of post-colonial countries today (see, for example, Mangan 1993). Postman and Weingartner in *Teaching as a Subversive Activity* wrote that 'it is generally assumed that people of other tribes have been victimised by indoctrination from which our tribe has remained free' (cited in Meighan and Siraj-Blatchford 1997: 356). This chapter was being written at the time of the build-up to the war against Iraq led by America and Britain. In one week's edition of the *Times Educational Supplement* at the height of the build-up to the war there was an article on nationalist ideological indoctrination in Iraq and the need for a post-war 'de-ideologicalisation' of the school curriculum. A few pages earlier was an article on the British government's policy to encourage faith-based state schools, i.e. schools based on religious ideology, indoctrination and social division (28/2/2003). Interestingly, the use of schooling to transmit religious beliefs (as opposed to education about such beliefs) is banned in South Africa (Carter *et al.* 2003: 21).

Three approaches or strategies to issues of schooling and group identity are often set out. The first is 'assimilation' where the burden is placed on those coming into the school to adopt the values and lifestyle of the existing dominant group in the school or the wider society, thereby reproducing this dominant position. Diversity is ignored on the assumption that all will conform to a given and established pattern of traditions, rules and structures. A 'multicultural' approach, on the other hand, recognises and even celebrates cultural difference and includes examples of diversity in the curriculum. However, this has been criticised for failing to address the use of power by one group to maintain or extend their socio-economic and political advantage over others by direct and indirect forms of discrimination. A third approach, 'anti-racism', builds on multiculturalism by acknowledging and analysing forms of power, prejudice and discrimination and actively challenging them through school rules and the curriculum. However, often missing from such debates is a very different stance to the three outlined above – the role of schooling in directly contributing to hatred of other groups, actively encouraging separation, prejudice and discrimination against them and even carrying out violence on the basis of inter-group hatred. This might be termed a 'pro-racist' strategy.

How can schooling be involved in such a strategy? The authoritarian nature of schooling and the stress on obedience to authority can provide a suitable setting not only for the reproduction of the group loyalties and hostilities of the surrounding societies but also the active encouragement and deepening of them. The film *Eye of the Storm* made in the 1960s portrayed the experiment carried out in a primary school in Iowa when the teacher split her class into blue-eyed children who were told that they were superior and brown-eyed children who were told that they were stupid and unattractive. Within hours the blue-eyed 'in-group' were bullying their classmates. This was deliberately used to raise issues of mutual respect and understanding amongst groups but was a clear indication of how it could be used in the opposite direction to indoctrinate hatred and fear. The combination of crude loyalty to a social group and unquestioning obedience to authority is a dangerous mixture. Unfortunately, although such experiments can help our understanding of how discrimination and inter-group hatred can be encouraged, we do not have to rely solely on experiments to understand the role that schooling can and does play. Schooling in Nazi Germany is an obvious historical example of the use of formal education systems to develop division and hatred but there are also more contemporary examples of schooling to demonise and dehumanise the 'other' or the 'enemy'.

In South Africa, for example, less than a decade before this book was written the entire country's education system was dedicated to preserving racial inequality and to creating mistrust and hostility between racial groups. Under apartheid in South Africa, expenditure on segregated education for the different officially defined racial groups was very unequal, with 'white' education being provided with far superior resources to 'black', 'Indian' or 'coloured' (Christie 1991). Schools' history textbooks taught about the 'superiority' of the whites, they devalued pre-colonial African societies, denigrated the role of black people in the building of South Africa and asserted the incapacity of black people to exercise political power and democratic rights (McKay 1995: 7; Dean *et al.* 1983: 103–104). Moreover, this attempt at racist indoctrination took place in schools and classrooms that were organised along authoritarian lines with regular use of corporal punishment (Harber 2001a: 19–21). A similar system existed in neighbouring Namibia until 1990. Chapter 3 discussed the difficulty of dealing with this legacy of racism in the post-apartheid education system and the tendency for racism to persist in schools through lack of deliberate intervention to combat it. However, while apartheid education in South Africa was probably the most systematic and well known example of the deliberate use of formal schooling to foster racism, unfortunately there are other contemporary examples.

Bosnia, Herzegovina and Kosovo

Following the dissolution of Yugoslavia the resulting states have emphasised and promoted ethnic nationalism as the basis for society. Part of this process has been the projection and fighting of an enemy 'other' as part of identifying who 'we' are. Schooling has been, and still is, used as an agent of socialisation in this process.

After the Balkan wars in the early 1990s the Dayton Peace Agreement of 1995 created an independent state consisting of two regions – the Federation of Bosnia and Herzegovina and the Republika Srpska. However, within this state the schooling system is divided into three along ethnic lines – Bosniak, Croatian and Serbian – and still fosters ethnic separation, distrust and hostility rather than dialogue and mutual respect and understanding.

An article on the Croat-Bosniak Federation in 1999 noted that schools often separate students based on their ethnicity, language and religion and schools exclude children from minority ethnic groups,

> In areas where the majority population is Croat, some Croat municipality heads lock the school doors in front of children and teachers of the Bosniak minority. In municipalities where the Bosniak population is in the majority, school leaders exclude attributes of the Croat nation and Croat culture from the school curriculum. Some Croat teachers and students refuse to attend schools with the Bosniak majority and would rather conduct class under tents, using curricula from neighbouring Croatia. There are many examples of lack of cooperation in the past three years. Although at the beginning of every school year solemn promises are made to solve the problems by the next school year, no real changes are made that prevent exclusion and separatist activity.
>
> (Pasalic-Kreso 1999: 2–3)

There have been a number of studies of school textbooks since the end of the war. Baranovic (2001) studied history school textbooks in all three education systems and concluded that,

> The existence of an ethnocentric focus was characteristic of all the textbooks analysed . . . By contributing more to the creation of a closed, ethnocentric identity of children, rather than to an identity open to diversity, history textbooks appear to function more as a disintegrative than integrative factor in the post-war reconstruction of social life in Bosnia and Herzegovina.
>
> (p. 24)

Heyneman and Todoric-Bebic (2000) argue that in a context where there is a long-standing tradition of authoritarian curriculum enforcement, it is natural that new, locally designed curricula may exacerbate rather than reduce tension. They use the ethnic bias and hatred in school history textbooks in Bosnia and Herzegovina as an example of this. They quote a section of a Bosniak text entitled 'Genocide and ethnic cleansing',

> Horrible crimes committed against the non-Serb population of Bosnia and Herzegovina by Serb-Montenegrin aggressors and domestic *chetniks* were aimed at creating an ethnically cleansed area where exclusively Serb people would live. In order to carry out this monstrous idea of theirs, they planned to kill or expel hundreds of thousands of Bosniaks and Croats. They had at their disposal the entire technical equipment of the Yugoslav National Army . . . The criminals began to carry out their plans in the most ferocious way. Looting, raping and

slaughters . . . screams and outcries of the people being exposed to such horrendous plights as the Bosniak people experienced . . . Europe and the rest of the world did nothing to prevent the criminals from ravaging and slaughtering innocent people.

(Heyneman and Todoric-Bebic 2000: 159)

The authors comment that whether this text is appropriate is not a matter of whether the events described occurred. Most important is that citizens from all different ethnic groups feel comfortable about the school curriculum – 'Bosnia needs a textbook policy that has criteria for approving the text-books to be used in all schools and which would not exacerbate the problems in the relationships with its neighbours' (Heyneman and Todoric-Bebic 2000: 160).

Davies (1999) describes in some detail the parallel but unequal Albanian/ Serb education systems that developed in Kosovo after the disintegration of Yugoslavia between 1990 and 1999. Each system was characterised by authoritarian organisation and teaching methods and each side perpetuated its own nationalistic myths and hatred of the 'other'. Crighton (2000: 2–3) provides some examples of this from history textbooks. Two are repro-duced here:

Young Serbs learn that: World War II proved the dignity of Serbian people who stood up to Hitler which led to genocide against Serbs by Croats, Germans, Bulgarians and Albanians; eventual partisan victory and the creation of the Second Yugoslavia were thanks to Serb blood.

Young Kosovar Albanians learn that: Kosovo between the two world wars experienced the darkest period in its history with more than 300,000 Albanians from Kosovo and Macedonia expelled to Turkey; World War II interrupted the deportations and ended the deliberate colonisation of Kosovo with Serbs; Albanian partisans fought hero-ically and liberated Albania in November 1944 without outside help. The fascist occupation of Kosovo was relative 'freedom' compared with Serb repression and deportations.

Young Serbs learn that: Until World War II Kosovo was the least developed region and it took enormous Serb and Yugoslav investment after the war to achieve Kosovo's prosperity. Nevertheless, after 1974 Kosovar Albanians terrorised Kosovar Serbs and the Yugoslav Federa-tion had to defend itself against Kosovar Albanian separatists.

Young Kosovar Albanians learn that: Agreements reached in 1943 to let Kosovo join Albania were not respected after the war and more than 250,000 Albanians were expelled to Turkey by Yugoslav security forces. After a long struggle, Albanian patriots succeeded in 1974 in making Kosovo an autonomous unit in the Yugoslav Federation. This autonomy was then removed by military force.

Crighton notes that after the ethnic cleansing, NATO bombing and massive refugee crisis of 1999 work was being done by UNICEF and non-governmental organisations to provide more balanced textbooks for the classroom and to purge books of inflammatory, misleading, tendentious and mythological content. However, she states that 'I am not optimistic about their success' (2000: 4).

Cyprus

Since 1974 Cyprus has been divided between the Turkish Cypriot north of the island and the rest of the island which is Greek Cypriot. Hostility between the two communities is exacerbated by schooling, and essays written for the author by Greek Cypriot students strongly suggest that this itself is facilitated by a centralised education system which allows teachers and pupils very little say in decision making. The following discussion concerns the role of schooling in the Greek Cypriot part of the island, though the sources cited below suggest that schooling plays a similar role in the Turkish Cypriot part of the island. An ethnographic study of identity construction among Greek Cypriot schoolchildren carried out by Spyrou (2002) in 1996–7 found that teachers would often turn to a nationalistic discourse in the classroom to explicate self-identity. On occasion they would use highly loaded and emotional language full of imagery such as the Turks 'slaughtering' the Greeks which portrayed an image of the Turks as ruthless murderers of innocent victims. During a class discussion about Egyptian civilisation in a geography lesson for fifth and sixth grades the teacher says 'From what we read were they (i.e. the Egyptians) people with civilisation? Were they, let's put it this way, barbarians like the Turks, the Ottomans, who have always been barbarians?'. In another lesson in Greek language with the fourth grade the teacher says 'How do you feel about the way they (i.e. the Turks) killed them (i.e. the Greek Cypriots), about the barbarous, barbarous way by which they killed them?', to which the student replies 'Mrs, the Turks don't have a heart'. Spyrou comments that,

> The negative construction of Turks in the classroom is, in the majority of cases, initiated and exemplified by teachers, though the children themselves may act as co-constructors during class discussion. Not all teachers, of course, share the same understandings and some of them do engage in alternative (more positive or less negative) construction of the Turks. But in their everyday practice many teachers find it easy to resort to the stereotypes that a nationalistic self/other frame

propagates, even when they themselves do not, in their understandings as individuals, support such a view.

(2002: 263)

For Spyrou, the Greek Cypriot teachers faced a fundamental dilemma of ethnic socialisation – how to instil in children a strong sense of national pride which they see as necessary for 'our' survival as a nation and for liberating 'our' occupied territories while simultaneously avoiding the demonisation of those who have occupied 'our' territories and are threatening 'our' survival? He argues that his data shows that in attempting to do the first many teachers refrain from doing the latter. This certainly seems to have at least some impact on the pupils. The children in schools described Turks as barbarians, bad, egoists, terrorists, torturers, warmongers, quarrelsome, rapists, wild, murderers, vandals, looters, heartless, revengeful, hateful, malicious, devious, ungrateful, unfair, jealous, illiterate, impolite, dirty, liars, foolish, crazy and thieves (Spyrou 2002: 264).

One Greek Cypriot woman wrote that,

> The children of Cyprus do not have it easy. On both sides of the barbed wire line that partitions the island, they are brought up on a mental diet of hate and propaganda. On both sides, in textbooks and teacher hand-outs, the message sounds depressingly similar: beware the terrible Turk, beware the grievous Greek. Such poison is hard to erase. As a teenager who grew up under the shadow of war in the former crown colony, I have yet to forget the slogan 'the good Turk is the dead Turk' two decades after it was drummed into me in the classroom.

The same article quotes a high school teacher who is an active peace campaigner,

> Usually whenever the word Turk or Turkish Cypriot is mentioned in state-school classes, they are automatically associated with an act of barbarism. I see it with my own children who blame everything from a natural disaster to a car-crash on the Turks. What we're essentially fighting here is the mask of the devil we have painted on the other's face.

(Smith 2002)

Germany

Since the fall of the Berlin Wall in 1989 racial attacks in the area of the former German Democratic Republic (GDR) have become commonplace and this is associated with the prevalence of neo-Nazism. Racist attacks take place between four and six times more often in the east than in the west. Less than 2 per cent of east Germany's population is from ethnic minorities whereas this figure is 10 per cent in the west. People from ethnic minorities are 25 times more likely to be attacked in the east than in the west. The usual explanation for this greater prevalence of neo-Nazism and racist attacks has been higher unemployment and limited opportunities for young people in the east. However, an alternative explanation is put forward by Christian Pfeiffer of the Lower Saxony Criminological Institute. He points out that 90 per cent of the perpetrators of racial attacks are not unemployed and that violent crimes are lower in the east than in the west generally – it is only when it comes to racially motivated crime that there is a particular problem in east Germany. He argues that the root cause of this is the education system.

In the former GDR the state's authoritarian education system placed too little emphasis on the personal development of children and too much on their integration into the system. As a result, people socialised in this system developed patterns of attitudes and behaviour that made them more susceptible to racism – basically, the more authoritarian the system, the more xenophobic the attitudes it produces. The education system in the GDR was based on discipline, order and cleanliness while creativity, individual expression and a culture of debate were neglected. As a result young east Germans feel threatened by anything alien. In addition the education system presented schoolchildren with an idealised picture of east German society and made the outside, capitalist world the scapegoat for its problems – a paradigm which some young east Germans now extend to 'foreigners'. He comments that 'If you incite schoolchildren to hatred of political opponents, you cannot be surprised when they transfer such concepts of an enemy to anything alien' and argues that although the education system disappeared over ten years ago, many of its worst aspects have been perpetuated by teachers and parents (Kundani 1999).

India and Sri Lanka

Schooling in India is currently involved in actively worsening inter-group relations and contributing to violence in two interconnected ways. First, in 2000 the government led by the Hindu nationalist Bharatiya Janata Party began to rewrite school textbooks to depict Muslims and Christians as alien villains. New textbooks were to defend the caste system and to contain a laudatory account of Hitler. One examination question in the state of Uttar Pradesh asked 'If it takes four savaks (Hindu religious workers) to demolish one mosque, how many does it take to demolish twenty?'. A social studies text in Gujerat describes the country's caste system as an ideal way of building society's social and economic structure and says of lower caste people 'Of course, their ignorance, illiteracy and blind faith are to be blamed for lack of progress because they still fail to realise the importance of education in life'. Other textbooks in Gujerat extol the superiority of the Aryan race. A new history and civics textbook claimed 'Aryans were the most illustrious race in history. They were a tall, fair complexioned, good looking and cultured people'. Another of the state's social studies books finds no space for describing Hitler's persecution of the Jews but claims 'he instilled the spirit of adventure in the common people' (Bates 2000b). Though liberal educationalists have tried to challenge the government in the Supreme Court, it is perhaps not surprising that there were communal clashes in Gujerat in March 2002 which affected schools and left more than 700 dead.

Violence against lower caste people or Dalits in India is widespread (Human Rights Watch 1999b). Schooling, however, not only exacerbates prejudice against lower caste people, it also acts in a directly violent way towards them. A national report in 2002 found that many lower caste children are regularly beaten at school by teachers who regard them as polluting the class. The caste definition of 'untouchable' was abolished in 1950 but the country's 200 million Dalits – now referred to as 'scheduled castes' or 'scheduled tribes' still routinely suffer discrimination. The India Education Report compiled by the National Institute of Educational Planning and Administration noted that lower caste pupils were verbally and physically abused. Teachers in schools often refused to touch them and made them targets of their anger and abuse. They were punished at the slightest pretext and often humiliated. They were made to sit and eat separately. Their exercise books or writing slates were not touched by the higher caste teachers. They were made to sit on their own mats outside the classroom or at the door. In many cases they are beaten up by children from the higher castes. Many lower caste children are not allowed to walk through the village on their way to school and are denied their right to free textbooks, uniforms and a midday meal. In rural Karnataka children from the lower castes are referred to as *kadu-jana* (forest people) by teachers who claim that they would not learn anything unless they were given a severe beating. Many teachers make them perform menial tasks like washing school utensils (Behal 2002c). In one particular case a 13-year-old Dalit pupil in New Delhi was beaten by her teacher for saying 'good morning'. When her father went to the school to protest, he too was beaten up and attacked by three teachers and was hospitalised as a result (Behal 2001a).

The two largest groups in Sri Lanka are the primarily Buddhist Sinhalese (74 per cent) and the primarily Hindu Tamils (18 per cent). A review of teaching materials used in Sri Lanka in the 1970s and 1980s (Nissan 1996) found that Sinhalese textbooks were scattered with images of Tamils as the historical enemies of the Sinhalese while celebrating ethnic heroes who had vanquished Tamils in ethnic wars. Ignoring historical facts, the textbooks tended to portray Sinhalese Buddhists as the only true Sri Lankans with Tamils, Muslims and Christians seen as non-indigenous and extraneous to Sri Lankan history (Bush and Saltarelli 2000: 13). There was no attempt either in texts used by the Sinhalese or by the Tamils to use positive illustrations of the other group. The texts were culturally inflammatory and laid the intellectual foundations for social conflict and civil war (Heyneman and Todoric-Bebic 2000: 155).

Israel and Palestine

School textbooks have been used by both sides in this conflict to vilify the other. In regard to Palestine, Velloso (1998) notes that after the 1967 war Israelis censored Palestinian textbooks, though that does not mean that other educational means were not used by Palestinian educators to instil feelings and opinions in schoolchildren. In books used before 1967 there were many hostile comments against Israel and Jews. After 1967 Palestinian children learned rhymes at school conveying violent messages concerning themes of patriotism, liberation through rebellion and hatred for Jews. In September 2000 the first textbooks written by Palestinians for children in the West Bank and Gaza were distributed to schools. These were immediately criticised by Israelis who said the books refused to recognise the Jewish state as a neighbour rather than confront it as an enemy. Israeli critics argued that the books deny Israel's right to existence, it does not appear on a map and it is portrayed as an illegitimate occupier (Goldenberg 2001).

However, research on Israeli textbooks cited in Velloso (1998) suggests that Israeli textbooks have emphasised the national unity of the people vis-à-vis an enemy – the Arabs. The Arabs are portrayed as inferior, primitive or backward and in stories were given labels such as 'bandits, wicked, blood-thirsty, murderers, gangs, or rioters'. The textbooks are used to justify the view that any violent action is justified in defending the state against the others (Arabs) who threaten it. Professor Daniel Bar-Tel of Tel Aviv University studied 124 elementary, middle and high school books on grammar and Hebrew literature, history, geography and citizenship. He concluded that Israeli textbooks present the view that Jews are involved in a justified, even humanitarian, war against an Arab enemy that refuses to accept and acknowledge the existence and rights of Jews in Israel. The early textbooks tended to describe acts of Arabs as hostile, deviant, cruel, immoral, unfair, with the intention to hurt Jews and to annihilate the state of Israel. Within this frame of reference Arabs were delegitimised by the use of such labels as robbers, bloodthirsty and killers. He pointed out that Israeli textbooks continued to present Jews as industrious, brave and determined to cope with the difficulties of improving the country in ways they believe Arabs are incapable of. Adir Cohen did research on 1700 children's textbooks published after 1967. He found that 520 of the books contained humiliating, negative descriptions of Palestinians. Sixty per cent of the 520 books refer to Arabs as violent; 52 per cent as evil; 37 per cent as as liars; 31 per cent as greedy; 28 per cent as two-faced and 27 per cent as traitors. Cohen points out that the authors of these books effectively instil hatred towards Arabs by means of stripping them of their human nature and classifying them in another category (Meehan 1999).

Dr Haggith Gor of the Centre of Critical Pedagogy in Tel Aviv argues that 'What schoolchildren get very strongly is Us versus Them'. Such attitudes are entrenched by viewing history through the lens of 2000 years of anti-semitism and by drawing on a message from the Nazi holocaust that is not so much about the need for tolerance as the need for strength (Goldenberg 2001).

Rwanda

> Neighbours hacked neighbours to death in their homes, and colleagues hacked colleagues to death in the workplaces. Doctors killed their patients and school teachers killed their pupils. . . .
>
> (Gourevitch 1998: 114–115)

During the colonial period in Rwanda the Belgian colonial government consistently favoured the Tutsi ethnic group over the Hutu ethnic group. The colonial education system in Rwanda actively discriminated against the Hutu majority and in favour of the Tutsi minority through the amount and levels of education provided and through stereotypes used in school textbooks (Bush and Saltarelli 2000: 10). Thus education contributed to and exacerbated the resentment and hostility between the two groups that began during the colonial period and finally erupted in the genocide of 1994 in which some 800,000 Rwandans, most of them Tutsis, died in 100 days. Little changed during the period of independence. The current government in Rwanda accuses the education system of having suffered from a 'colonial hangover', separating a small percentage of the population, who were educated to run the country, from the masses and, as the government's education policy statement says, 'The consequence of such an education was the genocide of 1994'. The education provided was traditional, teacher-centred chalk and talk (Woodward 2000). As one analyst of Rwanda put it, the violent massacre of Tutsis by Hutus was based on the 'total dehumanisation of the Evil Other and the absolute legitimisation of Authority'. Schools were a part of the authoritarian social and political system and played a part in the indoctrination of hatred and the killing itself – 'Schools could not be places of refuge either and Hutu teachers commonly denounced their Tutsi pupils to the militia or even directly killed them themselves' (Prunier, 1995: 142, 254). As one of the teachers told a French journalist,

> A lot of people got killed here. I myself killed some of the children . . . We had eighty kids in the first year. There are twenty-five left. All the others, we killed them or they have run away. The relations of targeted people were often killed too, simply because of the family connection.

So a relation's house was a trap rather than a place of safety and the presence of somebody who was being hunted would endanger any relation who might otherwise have been spared.

(Prunier 1995: 254–255)

Schoolchildren took part in the massacres and schools were sites of mass murder (O'Kane 2000).

Conclusion

Education ought to be about learning to respect others and to treat all human beings on a basis of having equal human rights. An appreciation of diversity while accepting the inherent humanity of all individuals should be the very essence of what it means to be 'educated'. Unfortunately, this is not always the case. While some schooling systems and individual schools do consciously attempt to combat group prejudices, negative stereotypes and discrimination, others do nothing and reproduce them while some actively perpetrate inter-group hatred, hostility and violence. People can leave these latter systems with formal qualifications at a high level but still be capable of holding violent and aggressive attitudes towards the other and of behaving in violent ways towards 'them' as well. We have seen the terrible results of this in the 'ethnic cleansing' and genocides in Rwanda and the former Yugoslavia. Formal education is not necessarily an innocent bystander in such events.

7 Schooling as sexual abuse

Girls continue to face many obstacles to learning. Safety within the school is an oft-cited, but perhaps less well understood, determinant of children's, especially girls', participation in basic education. As this report shows, violence towards girls in schools is pervasive and worldwide. An unsafe learning environment is among reasons that girls discontinue their studies or parents refuse to enrol and keep their daughters in school. Addressing school-related gender-based violence, however, cannot be limited only to girls. Boys are victims as well as perpetrators of violence.

(Katherine Blakeslee, Foreword to USAID 2003)

Introduction

Chapter 3 of this book discussed sexual violence by male pupils on female pupils in schools. This was a case of violence by omission, where the school ignored or condoned such activities and did not do enough to stop them. The present chapter is concerned in the first place with the role of schooling in direct forms of abuse – where school staff actually carry out the abuse themselves. A second concern will be with the role of schooling in reproducing and perpetuating models of masculinity predicated on violence, including sexual violence.

The World Health Organization has defined sexual violence as, 'any sexual act, unwanted sexual comments or advances . . . against a person's sexuality using coercion, by any person regardless of their relationship to the victim, in any setting, including but not limited to home and work' (2002: 149). The Gulbenkian Foundation defined child sexual abuse as 'actual or likely sexual exploitation of a child or adolescent. The child may be dependent and/or developmentally immature' (1995: 167).

As the World Health Organization notes, sexual violence has a profound impact on physical and mental health,

As well as causing physical injury, it is associated with an increased risk of a range of sexual and reproductive health problems, with both immediate and long-term consequences. Its impact on mental health can be as serious as its physical impact and may be equally long lasting. Deaths following sexual violence may be as a result of suicide, HIV infection or murder – the latter occurring either during a sexual assault or subsequently as a murder of 'honour'. Sexual violence can profoundly affect the social well-being of victims; individuals may be stigmatised and ostracised by their families and others as a consequence.

(2002: 149)

It also needs to be stressed that sexual relationships between teachers and pupils must always be considered abusive, even if the sex is consensual. Power and authority relationships between teachers and pupils are not equal and teachers have a professional responsibility to treat all pupils equally, which cannot be the case if sexual relations are taking place with certain individuals. Unfortunately, sexual abuse by teachers does occur in schools, primarily by male teachers against girls but also by male teachers against boys and very occasionally by female teachers against male pupils. This appears to be a widespread problem in sub-Saharan Africa, or at least the problem is well documented for that region, and a large part of the discussion of sexual abuse will focus on schools there. Within sub-Saharan Africa, the problem is particularly acute in South Africa and this country has a section to itself. The next section of the chapter, however, describes instances elsewhere. The purpose of this chapter is not to suggest that all schools everywhere are riddled with sexual abuse and violence by teachers, though in some contexts it does seem particularly prevalent, but that it does consistently occur internationally when it shouldn't happen at all. Moreover, it is the authoritarian, closed nature of much schooling meshed with patriarchal values and behaviours that provides a context in which the events described can happen.

International instances of teacher-initiated sexual abuse in schools

O'Moore and Minton (2003) note that until relatively recently in Ireland a great deal of educational provision was in the hands of members of religious orders. Instances of extreme physical violence under the guise of (authoritarian) classroom 'discipline' and sexual abuse went unreported or reports were disbelieved 'quite literally for generations'. They refer to a four-part series on RTE (the state broadcasting service) called *States of Fear* which featured harrowing accounts of abuse suffered by pupils at the hands of members of religious orders who ran the state's institutional schools. The programme, which began in April 1999, precipitated the disclosure of many other cases of abuse in institutional schools. By March 1999 legal proceedings had been initiated in 145 cases involving allegations of sexual or physical abuse of children while in institutions that were operated by or on behalf of the state. In Britain, Skinner (2001) analyses a range of actual situations of sexual abuse in schools. One analysis of sexual abuse at a private rural boys' boarding school in England focused on the relationships of domination and authoritarianism in the school that provided a context for such acts to happen (Jones 1994).

In Japan reports of sexual misconduct by teachers in schools rose tenfold between 1989 and 2000. An Education Ministry report said that the number of teachers disciplined for indecent behaviour towards students rose from 12 to 51 in 1999. Teachers accused of sexual harassment were either dismissed or suspended from work. Educationalists said that the sharp rise in reported assaults could be attributed to the fact that victims of sexual abuse are now more likely to come forward as taboos subside in Japan. They said that boards of education will have to become more willing to discipline teachers for unacceptable behaviour. A study conducted by the Tokyo public school teachers' union found that one-tenth of high-school girls say that male teachers have asked them to serve them tea or give them a massage and a similar number said that they were told to act more feminine. More than 10 per cent of the girls said teachers had stared at their bodies while a slightly lower percentage said that teachers had touched their bodies (Fitzpatrick 2000).

In India a headteacher was charged with abducting six of his pupils, including his own daughter, and trying to sell them into the sex trade. The girls, minors between the ages of nine and twelve, were rescued by the police after alarmed parents reported that their children had not come home from school. The police were quoted as fearing that this case was 'only the tip of the iceberg' (Behal 2001b). In Ontario, the largest state in Canada, an inquiry resulting in a 570-page report found that children being sexually abused by teachers are frequently ignored by the authorities. The investigation revealed that school boards routinely 'passed on the trash', allowing paedophiles to 'hunt again at another school' (Greenfield 2000). Fox (1999) reports that in Papua New Guinea fear of sexual harassment by teachers was one reason why female pupils refused to attend community boarding schools. In one province it was reported that some teachers had sexual liaisons with girls aged 10 to 11 and had paid parents not to report the incidents. In France police investigated accusations against a paedophile primary school teacher who admitted at least one of the accusations made against him. Amid accusations of a cover-up, the school's director and a former education inspector were questioned for not reporting the offences after they had been alerted. In September 1997 the then schools minister said it was time to finish with the 'culture of silence' and issued a circular reminding educational staff of their duty to report cases of abuse against pupils (Marshall 2001).

In terms of a different understanding of sexual abuse, the Turkish Ministry of Health ordered that virginity tests be performed on high school girls of 15 to 17 years old studying to be nurses or medical technicians at the country's medical high schools. The school authorities will be able to order a virginity test if they suspect 'prostitution or sexual activity'. Such examinations were earlier prohibited after a case in 1999 in which five girls took rat poison in order to avoid the test. Selahattin Gumus, from the teachers' union Egitem Sen, described the tests as 'completely against human rights – part of an outdated mentality that is sexist and chauvinist' (Gorvett 2001).

Sexual abuse by staff in formal education in sub-Saharan Africa

Sexual abuse by teachers in schools in sub-Saharan Africa needs to be set in a wider context of gendered violence. Professor Amina Mama of the University of Cape Town puts it that,

> It is no exaggeration to state that violence and its particular gender-based manifestation has become an integral feature of Africa's post-colonial societies. This is true, not just in the war zones of Somalia, Rwanda and Liberia but also in supposedly peaceful contexts, where the daily torture and abuse of women is not even included in discussions of the continent's crisis. Worse still, there is growing evidence that Africa's newest democracies, South Africa and Nigeria, are particularly dangerous places for women. In both these cases, gender-based violence appears to be accepted as a normal aspect of daily life . . . Simultaneously straddling modernisation with masculinist memory and nostalgia, African governments have often created and sustained the sexual and economic conditions of gender inequality that facilitate the abuse of women . . . As a result of their silence, tolerance remains enshrined in legal, policing and medical policies and practices. Where there have been significant legislative innovations and policies, these have not been implemented, nor has their implementation even been budgeted for . . . Gender-based violence is an integral aspect of modern African life, an invidious social ill that forestalls development, nullifying all the talk about women's rights and human rights and shooting democracy in the foot.
>
> (2000: 1–2)

A survey carried out by Africa Rights and cited by the World Health Organization found cases of schoolteachers attempting to gain sex in return for good grades in the Democratic Republic of the Congo, Ghana, Nigeria, Somalia, South Africa, Sudan, Zambia and Zimbabwe (WHO 2002: 155). Research in Ghana, Malawi and Zimbabwe carried out for the British Department for International Development and described by Leach (2001, 2002) found evidence of teachers making unsolicited sexual advances and other forms of inappropriate sexual behaviour. In Zimbabwe schools, the teachers appeared to pursue their amorous activities both inside and outside the classroom quite openly; in the classroom, boys and girls would whistle or hiss if a teacher called on a particular girl known to be of interest to him to read out loud or come in front of the class . . . Boys were loud in their condemnation of such teachers, not for moral reasons but because they saw it as unfair competition. The teacher was abusing his position of authority; the girls were their peers and therefore 'their property'.

(Leach 2002: 9)

Moreover, male teachers who behave in this way are indicating to boys that such behaviour is acceptable. Some key findings of the research were:

- Sexual abuse of girls by girls by male pupils and teachers is accepted along with corporal punishment, verbal abuse and bullying, as an inevitable part of much of school life. It exploits unequal power relationships and the authoritarian ethos within schools.
- The reluctance of education authorities to address the issue and to prosecute perpetrators allows abuse to flourish unchecked. By their inaction, authorities condone and encourage it.
- Sexual abuse of girls in school is a reflection of gender violence and inequality in the wider society. Domestic violence against women and children is commonplace, as is rape and forced sex within relationships. Women are considered as 'belonging' to men and hence accorded lower value and status.

A study of child abuse by teachers in secondary schools in Zimbabwe by Shumba (2001) was entitled 'Who guards the guards in schools?'. This refers to a previous study by the author showing that teachers do carry out sexual abuse and that the great majority of the victims were between 12 and 16 years old. Shumba recognises that the majority of pupils do not file complaints against teachers for fear of being victimised. He argues that only about 10 per cent of such cases get reported. Shumba nevertheless managed to get access to 212 perpetrator's files held by the Ministry of Education, even though these were the 'tip of the iceberg'. Of these, 99 per cent were male, of whom 82 per cent were trained teachers and 18 per cent were untrained. Not surprisingly, the article calls for an overhaul of the teacher education curriculum to deal properly with issues of sexual abuse and professional responsibility.

In an article on sexual harassment in African education, Hallam (1994–5) quotes a Somali woman who went to school in Mogadishu who described sexual pressure from teachers as 'widespread',

When male teachers made their intentions clear to female students and you refused, they had many ways of getting back at you. They would embarrass you in class, always picking on you to stand up and answer questions, to come to the blackboard and explain something to the whole class. Some teachers would banish you from their classes altogether and of course everyone would know the reason. Worse still, they would give you poor marks or fail you outright. I remember a girl in the final year of intermediate school. The history teacher pursued her relentlessly. She refused. He told her to choose between him and her final exams. She dropped out of school.

(p. 18)

Hallam adds that the absence of channels for reporting abuse when committed by teachers means that most cases of sexual violence and harassment go unreported. Many students fear that reporting harassment by a teacher will result in failure or expulsion, a price they consider too high.

Omale (2000) cites a number of cases of teachers getting schoolgirls pregnant in Kenya and of primary schoolgirls under pressure to sell sex to their teachers in exchange for better grades. At one primary school, girls complained about two teachers who beat them if they turned down their advances and especially if they reported the harassment to the school authorities. (The two teachers were subsequently 'punished' by being transferred to another school.) One assistant chief in north west Kenya reports a common practice of poverty-stricken families that have been wronged to accept compensation in cash or kind from the offending teacher or his family, 'They pay compensatory money and gifts to parents, knowing that they could land in a lot of trouble if the matter was brought before a court of law. So the matter ends there' (Omale 2000: 32).

Omale cites two cases from schools in Kitale. In the first case male teachers implicated in sexual harassment were still in post because of the overwhelming support from fellow male colleagues. During a disciplinary hearing a teacher asked to explain his conduct claimed that the girl in question had tempted him to molest her. No action was taken. In the second case a pupil who reported to the headmaster that she was being harassed by her teachers was shocked when the headmaster joined her harasser's bandwagon. She reported the matter to some female teachers who opted to return her to her parents for her own safety.

In Zambia the Director of the Copperbelt Health Education Project, a leading aid agency, said that up to one in five girls are sexually abused at school by their teachers. The stigma surrounding HIV/AIDS had made addressing the problem more difficult. In Zambia 1.2 million young people are already estimated to be HIV positive and children as young as six are most at risk in the one place they should feel safe – school. The Ministry of Education estimates that more that 1000 teachers a year die of AIDS yet staff are bribing students into sex by offering them illicit access to exam papers or buying them books or a school uniform (Spelvins 2002).

In Uganda a study of gender, power relations and culture in an élite school found that female teachers, especially younger ones, were harassed by both male pupils and teachers. Male teacher behaviour ranged from comments on the teacher's dress, whistling at a teacher on sight and writing statements about a teacher on the board (Mirembe and Davies 2001). In Ghana a study of newly qualified teachers found that issues of sexual abuse by teachers in rural areas regularly emerged unprompted in interviews with headteachers and the newly qualified teachers. Indeed, there is even a slang expression for the perceived incentive for male teachers of available sexual opportunities in rural areas – 'bush allowance' (Hedges 2002: 137).

USAID (2003: 9–12) provides a useful summary of some empirical studies of gender-based violence in schools in Africa. The following is a summary of some key findings. In Botswana, in one study of 800 students 38 per cent of girls reported that they had been touched in a sexual manner without their consent; 17 per cent reported having had intercourse, 50 per cent of which was forced; 34 per cent reported they had sex for money, gifts or favours and 48 per cent reported never having used a condom. In another study in Botswana 67 per cent of girls reported sexual harassment by teachers and 11 per cent of girls were seriously considering dropping out due to ongoing harassment by teachers. In a study of 1688 secondary school students in the Cameroon sexual abuse was reported by 16 per cent of the sample and 8 per cent of the attackers were teachers. In a study of 400 in-school and out-of-school adolescents in Ghana, teachers were 5 per cent of those listed as people who forced girls to have sex. In a study of 1219 schoolgirls in Tanzania 6 per cent reported sexual harassment by teachers as a common problem.

South Africa

> Statistical evidence tells us that South African women are more likely to be murdered, raped or humiliated than women anywhere else in the democratic world, including the rest of Africa.
>
> (Mama 2000: 3)

South Africa is a violent society. An average of 52 people were murdered each day in South Africa in 1995, giving it a murder rate more than 80 times that of Britain and making South Africa the most violent country in the world outside a war zone (*Weekly Telegraph* 20–24 April 1996). In the first eight months of the same year, 80 per cent of adults and 62 per cent of children faced some sort of violent crime (Morrell 1998). A number of factors have combined to cause this 'culture of violence' – over 40 years of gross economic and political inequality, the social dislocation caused by the physical removal of whole communities, violent repression by the apartheid state unavoidably resulting in violent resistance to it, the widespread availability of guns and patriarchal values and behaviours. Estimates vary for how often a woman is raped in South Africa from every 26 seconds to every 90 seconds. Rates of HIV/AIDS infection in South Africa are very high. A health department survey in KwaZulu Natal in 1998, for example, found that 35.2 per cent of the population was infected, with the bulk of the cases between 15 and 25 years old (Pillay 2000).

Schools are far from being immune from this sexual violence and indeed help to perpetrate it. In October 1997 the report of the Gender Equity Task Team on gender equity in education was published (Wolpe *et al.* 1997). This was the first of its kind in South Africa and is a lengthy document that provided an authoritative and comprehensive account of the state of affairs with regard to gender issues in South African education. On the back cover it states that 'South African education is riddled with gender inequities that impact negatively on girls and boys, women and men – but especially on the quality of life and achievements of women. These inequities exist throughout the system and include the extremely worrying elements of sexual harassment and violence'. This document, however, did not really examine the role of teachers in sexual abuse in any detail. However, in 2001 Human Rights Watch produced a detailed report entitled *Scared at School: Sexual Violence Against Girls in South African Schools*. This is based on research in KwaZulu Natal, Gauteng and the Western Cape. The report states,

> Based on our interviews with educators, social workers, children and parents, the problems of teachers engaging in serious sexual misconduct with underage female students is widespread. As the testimony offered below demonstrates, teachers have raped, sexually assaulted and otherwise sexually abused girls. Sometimes reinforcing sexual demands with threats of physical violence or corporal punishment, teachers have sexually propositioned girls and verbally degraded them using highly sexualised language. At times, sexual relations between teachers and students did not involve an overt use of force or threats of force; rather teachers would abuse their authority by offering better grades or money to pressure girls for sexual favours or 'dating relationships'.
>
> (Human Rights Watch 2001: 37)

Perhaps the most startling figure was provided by a Medical Research Council survey carried out in 1998 that found that among those rape victims who specified their relationship to the perpetrator, 37.7 per cent said their schoolteacher or principal had raped them (Human Rights Watch 2001: 42). As someone very familiar with South Africa, it took some time for this figure to sink in even with me. Section V of the report details many actual cases of sexual abuse carried out by teachers in schools. Section VII of the report describes how when girls reported sexual violence and harassment they encountered a pattern whereby schools failed to respond with any degree of seriousness:

> Girls were discouraged from reporting abuse to school officials for a variety of reasons, not the least of which was the hostile and indifferent responses they received from their school communities. Sometimes school officials appear to have failed to respond adequately because they simply did not know what to do; other times they ignored the problem; still other times they seem to have been afraid to assist. In many instances, schools actively discouraged victims of school-based gender violence from alerting anyone outside the school or accessing the justice system. In the worst cases, school officials concealed the existence of violence at their schools and failed to cooperate fully with authorities outside the school system . . . Despite statutory obligations to report child abuse, when a school employee is accused of committing sexual assault, a common response of school officials is to try to keep the problem within the school community by concealing the existence of abuse and shielding from scrutiny those alleged to have committed acts of sexual violence.
>
> (Human Rights Watch 2001: 71, 81)

Evidence from the Midlands area of KwaZulu Natal found a culture of silence surrounding gender violence in schools, despite this becoming a norm in 'black' urban and rural schools. Most teachers who violate girl children get away with it because victims do not report it as they are afraid of being blamed or victimised by parents and other teachers which, as the authors state, highlights an unhealthy over-respect for the teachers, and this perpetuates the myth that the person who was raped must have asked for it. In addition, parents do not report sexual harassment because they fear that the girl will be asked to leave school. Parents may even feel that monetary payment from the perpetrator is far more useful than lengthy trials and enquiries. In some cases the payment can be as little as 20 rand (less than £2.00) and parents are prepared to accept this (Mshengu and the Midlands Women's Group 2003).

Masculinity, violence and schooling

> Schools, clubs and colleges are institutions where gender is actively forged. Gender isn't just reflected or expressed. They are places where a certain type of 'top dog' masculinity is made, celebrated and confirmed through daily acts of violence and bullying.
>
> (Salisbury and Jackson 1996: 105)

Violent crime, including sexual violence, overwhelmingly is carried out by males and particularly young males. However, whilst most violence is carried out by men most men are not violent. Violent behaviour by males is not biologically determined by, for instance, high levels of testosterone. If it was then most men would be violent. The Gulbenkian Foundation made the following case against biological determinism of violence in males,

> First, one can point to the admittedly unusual societies in which the biologically normal females have shown a greater tendency to violence than the biologically normal males. Secondly, we know that boys brought up in non-violent households with parents providing good quality care and living in non-violent neighbourhoods, show levels of violence that are very little different from girls brought up in the same circumstances. Thirdly, there is evidence that the levels of testosterone in young violent males are no different from those in non-violent young males.
>
> (1995: 42)

Moreover, as Connell (2000: 22) notes, cross-cultural studies of masculinities reveal a diversity that is impossible to reconcile with a biologically fixed master pattern of masculinity.

So why is it that in many societies men are more disposed towards violence than women? The answer is in terms of learnt or socialised behaviour around what it means to be and act as a man. Although there are multiple forms of masculine identity within and between societies, there are also dominant or hegemonic forms of male identity internationally which have traditionally preserved patriarchal power and privilege. Among the characteristics of this hegemonic form of masculinity are misogyny, homophobia, racism, compulsory heterosexuality, the importance of sport, a denial of emotions, competition, success, individualism, strength, toughness and the threat or use of violence to get what is wanted or, often, what it is assumed the male is entitled to and has a right to. Boys or men who deviate from this model where it dominates can be seen, labelled and treated as 'unmanly' (Morrell 1998; Salisbury and Jackson 1996; Frank 1996). It is obviously a model of masculinity predicated on aggressive behaviour and a proclivity towards violence. As Salisbury and Jackson put it, 'men and boys aren't violent because they have male bodies. They are violent in order to become more masculine' (1996: 106).

What role does schooling play not only in reproducing this model by omission but in actively encouraging such potentially violent, macho models of masculinity? The first and most obvious point is that, for better or for worse, teachers are role models. Male teachers act as role models for male students. By being involved in sexual harassment and rape, male teachers in the contexts described in this chapter are actively encouraging their male pupils to behave in a similar manner.

Another point is that schools can actively encourage adherence to violent forms of masculinity by the messages that they teach. Najcevska (2000) examined school literature and history textbooks in Macedonia, most dating from 1995–7. History was designed as a collection of wars and revolutions rather than trends in culture, art and civilisation. The covert but undeniable message is that the rightful response to violence is more violence. In the textbooks men are actively portrayed as soldiers, fighters, enemies or defenders while women play a passive or absent role. In the literature books men are positively characterised as military leaders, fearless fighters, conquerors and leaders. The most frequent situations in which male characters are placed are revolt, tumult, hatred, freedom-loving, combat against tyranny, loyalty to the people proved even under torture. The characteristic roles in which masculinity is manifested are the rebel, the hero, the dreamer, the assassin, the suicide, the man of action, the fighter against tyranny and the super-patriot. Women, on the other hand, are portrayed as housewife, mother, girlfriend or sister. Their characteristics are to be tender, industrious, faithful, self-sacrificing, full of love for their children, careful, unselfish, noble, good-hearted, patient, obedient, sad and devoted. Violent struggle was therefore inseparably tied to masculinity.

She adds that these conclusions are especially important in the light of survey evidence that suggests that traditionalism is deeply rooted in the consciousness of the young people of Macedonia and this affects social attitudes and that there are gender differences in such attitudes that could be related to violence. Boys, for example, more freely expressed hatred towards other nationalities and girls are more likely to claim to have no such hatred.

Salisbury and Jackson (1996) identify a number of ways that schools actively perpetuate forms of masculine identity that lend themselves to violent interpretation. Although writing primarily of a British context, the aspects they identify are common features of schooling internationally and reflect major themes of the analysis of schooling that has been presented in this book so far, but from a gender perspective. First, they argue that the way that schools are organised – their authority patterns and forms of discipline – reinforce key aspects of the hegemonic masculinity outlined above, which is why men have traditionally dominated school management,

> Teaching is seen to be about control and authoritarian certainty. It is also the visible face of material male power in the establishment. The characteristics of effective teaching become talking from the front and controlling any child's responses. It is also about a system of duties, patrolling corridors and the constant checking of students' presence. The atmosphere of control will be underpinned by the need to impose a strong, hard, authoritarian disciplinary system . . . Many male teachers maintain their authority over pupils by a 'hard-line' rule of fear. They control by threats and a loud voice to reduce students to frightened silence. From such an aggressive disciplinary style boys learn

that 'this is how you get what you want'. Male teachers are also very competitive around their ability to establish firm discipline. There is ridicule of 'soft' members of staff behind their backs. . . . Boys learn to expect dominant authoritarian behaviour from male teachers since it provides a role model for superior power and strength. It mirrors much of the power they see exhibited by other men in their daily lives – their fathers, brothers, uncles and grandfathers.

(1996: 18, 22, 28)

Second, the curriculum is seen as 'academic masculinist' in that knowledge is presented as abstract, neutral and value free,

School knowledge retains the academic form of a self-referring, abstract body of knowledge which strongly separates what is learned from the personal and social experiences of the learner. Knowledge is also orga-nised hierarchically from the less difficult to the more difficult. This emphasises the idea of there being one path through the material which is necessary to follow. The way knowledge is imparted is by means of transfer teaching i.e. something the teacher knows is trans-ferred to the mind of the student, i.e. a 'delivery' model. This still occurs by means of chalk and talk and teaching from the front so that impersonal science demands an impersonal teaching style with no attempts to link what is done with the lives of children. Links with students as people are superficial because of the way teachers know their subject and desire to impart subject knowledge. Knowledge control and what needs to be known is in the hands of men.

(Salisbury and Jackson 1996: 25)

While alternative forms of knowing can be found in schools, the above form tends to be taken more seriously. An interesting example of this is provided by Hutchinson (1996: 113–114) in relation to Australia. A national curricu-lum mapping study was conducted by the directors of curriculum from the various school systems across the country. In the eight state systems func-tional literacy in reading and writing, numeracy and computer literacy were consistently given high priority while social literacy/problem solving skills/social living skills/conflict resolution skills was given medium priority in four states and low priority in the other four.

Third, Salisbury and Jackson argue that closely allied to this curriculum is the way learning is organised and tested. The emphasis on individual competition is closely linked with patriarchal values. They argue that, 'Competition brings up many kinds of unpleasant feelings, such as being pushy and arrogant around winning and sneakily resentful around failure' (1996: 31).

While competition and testing and the resulting stress and illness is the major theme of the next chapter, here the important point is that exams, league tables and competition 'activates the notion of manly values around winners and losers' and,

> that not to shape up properly as a boy in competition with others causes pain, resentment and anti-social behaviour in the form of truancy, disruptiveness and other attention-grabbing devices. After all, a competitive system that fails some boys academically and physically compels a compensatory assertion of masculine pride, a competition in machismo to enable male power to be demonstrated and admired.
>
> (Salisbury and Jackson 1996: 32)

A fourth way in which schools reinforce hegemonic models of masculinity is through sport. Playing sport in a manly way means a determination to win at all costs by gritting teeth and ignoring the hurt of physical clashes,

> The language of school sports for many boys is the language of warfare – 'Hit them hard today, lads!' All the talk is of combat, battles, seeing your opponent as the enemy and military conquest. There is a gladiatorial type of imagery of sparring, grappling and not deserting your post. The results of this sport-as-welfare approach is often to normalise aggressive competitiveness in the lives of many boys.
>
> (Salisbury and Jackson 1996: 205)

Frank's study of boys in Canada reached similar conclusions,

> Tied as it is to the frequently brutal features of patriarchal culture such as misogyny, violence, sexism and heterosexism, sport for these boys was much more than an 'innocent' pastime played for fun. Their sport activities helped to maintain inequality between and among these young men along divisions of physical size and strength, class and sexual orientation. The accompanying violence – often accepted and celebrated by many staff and coaches within the school – created apprehension, fear, low self-esteem and self-loathing for some of the boys. They never seemed to be able to measure up.
>
> (1996: 117)

Skelton's (1993) autobiographical account of physical education teachers in Australia suggests that there is an occupational culture that centres on conventional or dominant forms of masculinity and that this is seen as natural, good, expected and taken for granted.

Conclusion

Schools are not necessarily safe places for girls. Sexual harassment and violence can come directly from teachers. Campaigns in developing countries to get more girls into school need to be balanced by attempts to change what can actually happen in them. Those boys and men that do behave violently towards females and indeed other males do not do so because of their biology. Violent forms of masculinity seem to be learned behaviour and unfortunately schooling seems to play a part in this. Kenway and Fitzclarence summarise the negative role of schooling in regard to masculinity well, again making connections with other themes discussed in the present book,

> If schools implicitly subscribe to and endorse hegemonic versions of masculinity, particularly in their more exaggerated forms, then they are complicit in the production of violence. If they fear 'the feminine' and avoid and discourage empathetic, compassionate, nurturant and affiliative behaviours and emotional responsibility and instead favour heavy-handed discipline and control then they are complicit. If they seek to operate only at the level of rationality and if they rationalise violence then they are complicit. If they are structured in such a way as to endorse the culture of male entitlement and indicate that the needs of males are more important than those of females then they are complicit. If they are repressive in their adult/child relations and do not offer adolescent students in particular opportunities to develop wise judgements and to exercise their autonomy in responsible ways then they are complicit. If they operate in such a way as to marginalize and stigmatise certain groups of students then they are complicit.
>
> (1997: 125)

8 Schooling can make you ill
Stress, anxiety and examinations

People in positions of influence seem to have forgotten that the best things in education are often those that cannot be measured.
(Headteacher of Millfield School in Somerset, UK bemoaning the British government's obsession with school league tables – *Times Educational Supplement* 17/10/2000)

Introduction

How many people do you know who still have unpleasant dreams about examinations even many years after taking them? Schooling's relationship with higher education and the labour market has meant that it has always been associated with competition, selection and measurement and this has had an effect on the individuals concerned in terms of worry, stress and anxiety. Stratified forms of school provision have prepared children for a stratified labour market. Both élite and mass forms of provision have been predominantly authoritarian, as has been argued in this book, but both have been competitive as well. In some societies this mixture of control and competition has now reached epidemic proportions, however, with serious effects on the health of children. This can be for different reasons.

In some societies the introduction of neo-liberal markets into schooling in order to increase government control through greater 'accountability' has resulted in an escalation of testing, not for the diagnostic benefit of learners but so that schools, education authorities, governments, countries and even individual teachers can be measured, ranked and judged to provide market information and therefore market 'choice' to parents. Just as it is possible to have 'failing' pupils so it is possible to have 'failing' schools, governments, countries, authorities and teachers (e.g. Apple 2001). At the same time, over the last 20 years or so some industrialised societies have become markedly less equal in terms of wealth while the importance of private wealth and the need for individuals to compete for it has been stressed by politicians. In other societies there is a cultural tradition of fierce competition within schooling and this has been exacerbated by neo-liberal market reforms. In developing countries the competition for scarce places in secondary and higher education, with their assumed links to the middle and upper levels of the labour market, has become exaggerated by cutbacks in public provision of education caused both by poor economic performance and by World Bank imposed structural adjustment programmes based on neo-liberal economics (Samoff 1994; IJED 1996; Reimers 1994).

Schooling is now therefore even more of a competitive assessment and selection mechanism with 'winners' and 'losers' at all levels. While competition does not necessarily lead to violence against children in a linear fashion, the avoidable consequence of this is the over-emphasis on testing and examinations, which is causing unacceptable levels of physical harm to pupils (and to teachers). In Britain, where the writer is based, it has reached particularly serious levels, so this chapter will begin there before discussing other national settings. The chapter will end with a discussion of the increased emphasis on assessment in relation to notions of modernity.

Britain

> A system that is prepared to examine six and seven year olds to further its own political agenda is sick.
>
> (Headteacher of Lymington Church of England infants schools, Hampshire, England quoted in the *Times Educational Supplement* 9/5/2003)

Estimates vary about how many official tests British children sit before they leave school but they all agree that there are a lot of them. Professor Colin Richards of St Martin's College, Cumbria estimated that most primary school children take more than 30 tests before they are 11 years old. High achieving students will take more than 40. He thinks that British children are the most heavily assessed in the world and asks 'What must it be like for low-performing children to be given 19 or 34 reminders of their performance?' This also means a large amount of class time preparing for the tests (Hackett 2001). One survey found that one in seven primary schools had begun revision in November for the tests for 11-year-olds the following June/July as teachers were under pressure to make sure their schools did well in league tables (Ward *et al.* 2002). By the end of secondary school it is estimated that pupils will have taken 105 official tests and exams during their school years. It is also estimated that secondary aged children are out of lessons for about 46 weeks of their seven years of secondary education because of the test system and spend something like 150 hours sitting exams. The annual cost of examinations is £200 million, a total which has risen 50 per cent since 1997 (Berliner 2003). It has to be remembered that the primary purpose of much of this testing is not diagnostic – it is not there to help the child – it is there so that schools, cohorts and government policies can be ranked and judged.

What is the result of all this testing on British children? One survey of more than 8000 secondary school pupils in England and Wales in 2000 led to a report entitled *Tested to Destruction*. The report claimed that stress is damaging teenagers' physical and emotional well-being. It claimed that children suffer severe stress from the endless tests. Physical symptoms included difficulty with sleeping and eating disorders such as bulimia and anorexia. A cartoon attached to the article describing the survey has a child returning home from school and saying to her mother 'We had a lesson in the break between tests today' (Smithers 2000b). More than a third of 7-year-olds suffer stress over national tests and one in ten lose sleep because they are worried about them according to a poll of 200 parents. The pressure starts in infancy and increases as children move through the school. By the age of 11, two-thirds of children show signs of stress as they revise for national tests. Around 34 per cent suffer from general stress, a quarter have lost confidence and 20 per cent are so busy revising they have no time to play with their friends. More than one in ten children have been reduced to tears in the run up to the tests, 12 per cent of 11-year-olds have refused to go to school to sit tests and 9 per cent have suffered anxiety attacks (Ward 2003a). There is also evidence that the testing regime coupled with league tables is forcing children to come into school even though they are sick (Ward 2002). Researchers from a psychotherapy unit at City University in London carried out 200 interviews and found 'worryingly high' levels of stress among children – nearly a quarter of under 18s said they often got stressed and only one in six never suffered from stress. A major source of this stress was the level of compulsory testing. In the article reporting this the National President of the Professional Association of Teachers is quoted as saying that young people are treated 'like products on a conveyor belt' (Burke 2000). Childline, a phone line which children can call for help, receives 800 calls a year from pupils suffering from stress. Childline's director for Yorkshire and the north east of England said that children often see failure as catastrophic for their future – 'They tell us that if they don't pass this, there is nothing else in life'. They come to see exams as the only measure of their worth (Williams 2003). A long-term study of the mental health of Scottish children carried out by the Medical Research Council revealed that psychological stress had increased significantly since 1987 and that there was a clear link with academic pressure as the levels of distress rose just before exams (Kirkman 2003). Moreover, studies of secondary school pupils have found that at the same time that they are struggling with the pressure of exams, nearly a third are dealing with life burdens (e.g. caring for sick relatives, death in the family, parental redundancy and moving house) that affect their results (Harris 2001).

The opposition Liberal Democrat education spokesman said that children aged five or five and a half are being referred to the doctor because of stress as they prepare for the national curriculum tests. He said, 'It is ironic that just as we are understanding the importance of free-range farming, we are turning too many of our nursery schools into little more than cages of battery hens' (Mansell and Bloom 2002).

The *Guardian* newspaper Education supplement provided an interesting case study of one sixth former. She has a working week that spreads across seven days and she works in excess of 50 hours, more than the average adult. She had to give up ballet, Saturday morning music school and swimming because she has no leisure time for them. She has no time to get herself a job for some financial independence or to read books outside the ones set for her courses. She also finds it difficult to sleep because she has too much on her mind and in early 2003 collapsed in the street from exhaustion. The article commented,

> Little wonder that reports of sixth formers needing medication for depression and panic attacks are growing . . . talk to teachers and you hear stories of young people falling ill because of stress, dropping out because of it or behaving badly because of it. Talk to teenagers and they will tell you of outside interests that have had to go, and how tired and grouchy they get because of the amount of homework they have to do staying up into the early hours finishing the coursework . . . (pupils) are being churned slowly through an educational sausage machine that threatens the physical and mental health of some, without any concomitant returns in a more rounded education.
>
> (Berliner 2003)

Katarina Tomasevski, special rapporteur on the right to education for the UN Commission on Human Rights, said that she believed the British government was in technical breach of the UN Convention on Children's Rights by imposing a targets and testing regime that ignores their needs. Whereas Article 29 of the convention says that education should be 'directed to the development of the child's personality, talents and mental and physical abilities to their fullest potential', she argued that the system of tests at 7, 11, 14 and 16 was designed to fulfil government objectives rather than meet the needs of children. Children were tested so much that she wondered whether the government wanted England to 'become another Singapore' – where in a poll pupils aged 10 to 12 said that they worried more about failing their exams than their parents dying (Woodward 2003).

If it isn't stress that causes physical damage, then school can be physically damaging in other ways. A study by a physiotherapist of 200 12- to 14-year-olds in Devon found that half of those who responded had suffered lower back pain and that they complained that this was the result of carrying heavy bags between classrooms as many schools no longer provide lockers or personal desks (*Times Educational Supplement* 21/8/2002). Handy's analysis of schools as prisons referred to in Chapter 2 notes that one aspect of this is that pupils have no space to call their own. A study of 11- to 14-year-olds carried out by Surrey University in Surrey and the north west of England found that around half of all children face a lifetime of back problems caused by poorly designed classrooms and bad posture in front of computer screens. The Professor of Ergonomics at Surrey said, 'The workforce of tomorrow is already damaged before starting the rigours of adult life' (*Times Educational Supplement* 13/9/2002).

While the main focus of this book is on the violent impact of schooling on pupils, it also has to be remembered that the general context of tests, inspections and league tables is also very stressful for teachers, who themselves become ill and there are many articles in the British educational press to this effect – as well as a number of articles on headteachers and other teachers who help their children to cheat because of the pressure on them caused by exams, league tables and the culture of target setting. This level of stress is obviously not good for the teachers concerned but it can also have repercussions for pupils. Of course, as a book by a deputy headteacher which examined evidence on stress in teaching in Britain put it, 'The basic model of a class, with one individual trying to persuade, or force, a number of other individuals to do things that left to themselves they would rather not do, has stress built into it' (Cosgrove 2000: 49). Moreover, as the same author goes on to say,

> If a teacher is suffering, the children in his or her care will suffer. Teachers debilitated by stress and unable to give of their best will be short-changing the pupils through no fault of their own . . . one way for an individual to cope with stress is to take it out on other people. We have all known the 'kick the cat' syndrome, when in frustration and anger a person lashes out at the nearest available target . . . Place a person under stress in a classroom with small children and the consequences will certainly be unpleasant and could be dire . . . Fortunately, physical attacks on children are rare, but the daily classroom experiences for a child whose teacher is under stress will certainly be less than positive. Shouting, verbal put-downs, short temper, poor quality assignments, poorly planned, unimaginative lessons, work not marked . . .
>
> (Cosgrove 2000: 117–118)

A study of disadvantaged children in two counties in England found that, apart from the children finding schooling a 'deeply boring experience', they also recognised that the pupils recognised that often when teachers humiliated or intimidated them or were verbally abusive it was because of tensions in the classroom caused by the difficult and stressful nature of teaching as a job (Riley and Docking 2002).

Stress as an international issue in schooling

While the situation may be particularly serious in Britain, stress and illness is also a major problem elsewhere. In Germany, the Bavarian Teachers' Federation warned of an alarming rise in the number of primary pupils taking medication for stress or simply to improve school performance. One in five primary children in Germany is taking medication for these reasons according to surveys carried out by health authorities in southern Germany. These findings have been borne out by studies carried out elsewhere in Germany. Dr Klaus Hurrelmann, Professor of Preventative Medicine at the University of Bielefeld's Public Health Faculty, estimates that as many as one in three pupils aged 5 to 9 take pills for stress. The medication is often bought over the counter by parents concerned about their children's performance at school and to combat sleeplessness, lack of appetite, headaches and stomach aches – classic symptoms of stress – as well as to improve concentration. Medication includes growing use of Ritalin (available only on prescription) to aid concentration, psychotropic mood-altering drugs, tranquillisers which are often addictive and codeine or caffeine-based stimulants. Hamburg University's clinic for child and adolescent psychiatry found in a study of 2000 families across Germany that one in five children between the ages of four and 18 needed therapy for psychological problems, often induced by stress over school performance. The Bavarian Teachers Federation found that primary school pupils today are more concerned about exams and marks than in the past, as post-school academic qualifications are seen as more important than a decade ago when many were happy to obtain industrial apprenticeships and learn a trade. Pressure at the age of ten, when many pupils face exams to determine entry to selective grammar schools, is cited as another factor and high parental anxiety is transferred to children (Sharma 2001b).

In America Denise Clark Pope (2001) carried out research on pupils' views of schooling in what is widely considered to be a 'good' high school with caring teachers, innovative programmes and strong leadership and where 95 per cent of the pupils go on to higher education. While there is evidence of success everywhere in the school,

> Listen to the students, though, and you'll hear a different side of success. To keep up her grades, Eve sleeps just two to three hours each night and lives in a state of constant stress. Kevin faces anxiety and frustration as he attempts to balance the high expectations of his father with his own desire to 'have a life' outside the school. Michelle struggles to find a way to pursue her love for drama with compromising college prospects. And both Teresa and Roberto resort to drastic actions when they worry that they will not maintain the grades they need for future careers. All of them admit to doing things that they're not proud of in order to succeed in school.
>
> (Pope 2001: 3)

The students explain that they are busy at what they call 'doing school'. They realise that they are caught in a system where achievement depends more on 'doing' – going through the correct motions – than thinking deeply, engaging in discussion or investigating topics which interest them. One of the students she studied says, 'People don't go to school to learn. They go to get good grades which brings them to college, which brings them the high-paying job, which brings them to happiness, or so they think. But basically, grades is where it's at' (Pope 2001: 3).

Values normally espoused in school such as honesty, diligence and teamwork necessarily come into question when the students have to choose between them and getting top grades. Passion and engagement were rare and the daily grind of the school day took its toll on health and happiness,

> Some of the students, like Teresa and Michelle, suffered frequent colds and illnesses due to such a harried pace, a lack of sleep and poor eating habits. Others, like Eve and Berto, who studied 'every minute' experienced great stress that led to anxiety, stomach problems, even a possible ulcer (for Eve). These students wished they could get more hours of sleep and improve their health, but their busy schedules, including school, family, and work obligations did not allow this change.
>
> (Pope 2001: 155)

The teachers too, 'seemed trapped by the realities of an overcrowded, impersonal, bureaucratic and competitive school system. There were too many students to get to know, too many individual needs to be met, and too little time, money, or support from administrators to accomplish . . . goals' (Pope 2001: 161).

The Junior Girl Scouts of America have introduced a stress management badge. By 2002 more than 60,000 girls had passed the badge's ten tests which teach the children how to cope with rising anxiety. They are now entitled to wear the fingernail chewers' emblem on their sleeves, alongside the more usual ones for things like making biscuits and map readings. The girls are between eight and eleven (*Independent on Sunday* 9/6/2002).

In 2003 plans were announced in America to put 908,000 four-year-olds through a 'battery' of tests by extending the testing regime from 5- to 18-year-olds to infants attending the government's free childcare facilities for the neediest families. The co-ordinator of early childhood education at North Seattle Community College said that the last time testing of this age group was tried in 1987 half the children were too scared to even function (Phillips 2003a).

In South Korea the education system has been described as 'examination hell'. Historically the school curriculum and teaching methods have been dominated by examinations. The existence of fierce competition, especially for college entrance, has meant that educators are under pressure to feed their students only the knowledge and skills needed for the tests. For the majority of students and teachers schooling has been nothing more than the cramming of knowledge into the heads of students. There is little or no room to respond to the diversity of interests and capabilities among students. To deal with the pressure of examinations, schools have set up programmes of autonomous (self) study and supplementary classes. In some schools this is compulsory and done under the supervision of a teacher, either an hour before school begins or after school, sometimes until 9 pm or midnight. Thus, teachers often work up to 12 hours a day. As the authors who describe this note, 'This situation has been extremely difficult for teachers and students' (Ko and Apple 1999: 67). Kang writes that in South Korea,

> Students at all levels are forced to compete against each other. Universities are ranked according to their social prestige and are very difficult to get into. Many students attend expensive schools after regular school hours to give them a competitive edge. All children are thus subject to severe pressure. One's success means another's defeat. Some desperate teenagers commit suicide.
>
> (2002: 322)

Adolescent suicide does indeed seem to have become a major problem in South Korea. One study in the 1980s showed that suicide accounted for 13.14 per cent of all deaths and was the second leading cause of death among youths aged 15 to 24. The youth suicide rate rose from 22.96 per 100,000 in 1981 to 28.62 per cent in 1983 and the youth suicide rate was higher than the national rate. The authors of the article from which these figures are drawn state that, 'The focus on educational achievement in contemporary Korea may now put great social pressure on adolescents in terms of their school performance. This may lead to stress and sometimes suicide' (Juon *et al.* 1994: 663). In discussing their findings on suicidal behaviour among Korean adolescents they further state that,

> Academic stress was associated with suicidal behaviours. Those students who felt stress concerning academic performance were more likely to have serious thoughts of suicide and attempt suicides than those who did not feel stress. Academic performance is of great importance in Korean society. In a longitudinal study of Korean adolescents to examine the effects of school failure on delinquency and psychological distress, Juon (1992) showed that school failure was associated with psychological distress and delinquent behaviours (i.e. failed students reported more distress and delinquent behaviours than successful students).
>
> (Juon *et al.* 1994: 673)

In 2003 in Egypt poor results in the final secondary school exam caused a spate of suicides. At least nine adolescents killed themselves either in anticipation or in consequence of low scores on the exam which determines admission to university. With a rising population and unemployment a degree is viewed by many young Egyptians as the only guarantee of a stable future and middle class families spend a lot of money on tutors (Lindsey 2003).

In India education officials have demanded an overhaul of the marking system and curriculum to tackle the growing problem of stress. In 2000, as in preceding years, at least four suicides by failing students were reported. The Central Board of Secondary Education was so concerned that it set up a round-the-clock help line staffed by volunteers to deal with pre-examination stress. Fifteen counsellors were operating in Delhi alone. However, demand did not fall after the exams ended and the lines had to be kept open to deal with anxious students waiting to see if they had got into college. The chief controller of examinations said that the pressure on students is made worse by parents who insist that children score the highest marks in every subject to secure admission to the best colleges. Some colleges make matters worse by having unrealistically high cut-off percentages. In some cases scoring 97 per cent in maths might not be enough for a student to go to their chosen college. One person who runs a help line said that at least 20 per cent of the calls were from students 'on the verge of suicide'. In Delhi in 1997 there were 30 examination suicides which prompted a major protest. In 1998 the figure was nine, in 1999 four and 2000 just one, so in Delhi at least the help lines seemed to have helped. Students in the rural areas do not have access to telephone help lines (Behal 2000). However, a report for India's National Council for Educational Research and Training found that three-year-olds are carrying up to 11 textbooks in their school bags and do at least one hour's homework a night. While primary schools are debating how to reduce the academic burden on children, middle-class parents are demanding more homework for pre-school infants so that they are better prepared for admissions tests to good schools (Behal 2003).

Testing, stress and modernity

In an article on relaxation training with children in schools the authors baldly state that 'Given the high prevalence of stress-related problems among school-aged children, pastoral care and student well-being remain primary concerns for psychologists and teachers' (King *et al.* 1998: 54). They then go on to discuss the usefulness of relaxation techniques in schools. However useful these and other techniques are, this is tackling the symptom not the cause. While pupils may well be stressed for reasons that lie outside of the school, there is no doubt that school's role in assessment and testing is contributing significantly to pupil stress and making them ill. Why do schools test more and more?

As Broadfoot argues,

> We live in a world obsessed with data; with the collection and dissemination of performance indicators, statistics, measures, grades, marks and categories. In a world in which it is assumed that quality can be defined, compared and certified. And a world in which what cannot be perceived, explained and measured is deemed either unimportant or non-existent, so that measurement not only dominates the means we choose to achieve our ends but the end itself.
>
> (2000: 199)

Broadfoot argues that this growing domination of assessment and measurement is the result of a belief in 'modernity' – a belief in the power of science and rationality to lead to social and economic improvement,

> Thus it is possible to link the steadily increasing significance of the role of educational assessment with the modernist project more generally and its domination by notions of rationality. The paraphernalia of modern systems of management – such as planning, quantification, accounting of revenues, outcomes, performance review, productive and societal contribution – all these are symptoms of modernity . . . The mechanisms used to define quality – typically marks, grades or levels – acquire a significance and a degree of trust which belies their fundamentally social origin.
>
> (2000: 204–206)

This is despite assessment being a process 'shot through with human subjectivity' (p. 209). Integral to this argument is that the modernist emphasis on assessment and measurement is a form of undemocratic control and discipline. She quotes Reimer (1971: 19) to the effect that,

> School has become the universal church of a technological society, incorporating and transmitting its ideology, shaping men's minds to accept this ideology and conferring social status according to acceptance. There is no question of man's rejecting such technology. The question is only one of adaptation, direction and control. The role of the school teacher in this process is a triple one of combining the functions of umpire, judge and counsellor.

One British National Health Service counsellor who writes extensively on psychotherapy, counselling and education argues that stress and ill health among teachers and pupils is a pathological symptom of technocratic modernity in education. In an article entitled 'Stress, surveillance and modernity', House (2000) expresses his own views, and in support of his arguments provides a useful review of Alan Block's (1997) book which is subtitled 'Education as the Practice of Social Violence against Children'. House himself argues that,

> an education system that is saturated with the values of unbalanced cognitive intellectualism, anxiety-provoking surveillance, a crassly super-ficial definition of 'standards', didactic compulsion of both teachers and pupils and infantilising deprofessionalisation cannot but be an unmiti-gated disaster for our obsessively monitored teachers and relentlessly over-tested children.
>
> (2000: 1)

Block argues that schools define children by the spirit of modernity, a period when order and classification were prioritised as values that defined the world. He sees modernity as a product of a human quest for certainty with technologies of measurement making the possibility of the achievement of certainty attainable. This is a world organised by the creation of order by the rational sciences and privileging manipulation, management and engineering. It is a world that denies ambivalence, doubt and uncertainty. Within education the attempt is made to control ambivalence and unpre-dictability among children, 'The child is . . . conceptualised as the empty vessel into which the state might pour its standardised materials . . . [such that] schools are organised to eliminate childhood . . . [with] standards [having] little to do with the child but rather what that child must become' (Block 1997: 129).

This control through regularisation, categorisation and the imposition of knowledge that must be learnt damages children through removing imagi-nation, creation and the importance of emotions and relationships as well as directly through the high levels of stress and anxiety described above. Moreover, as House argues, when children rebel against this imposed order they are diagnosed as having 'attention deficit disorder' and can be prescribed powerful and potentially damaging drugs such as Ritalin, even though the extent to which attention deficit disorder actually exists as a medical diagnosis or a convenient social construct to control deviant beha-viour is a matter of some controversy (Ideus 1994).

Conclusion: testing, competition and aggression

Kohn (1993: Chs 8 and 11) provides a detailed critique of the regular use of tests and grades using research evidence to support his argument that they demotivate pupils, harm the nature of learning that takes place, encourage cheating, damage the relationship between the teacher and learner and induce blind conformity. However, competitive testing on the scale and intensity described above is not only not good educational practice but is also a form of violence against many pupils because it harms them directly both physically and emotionally. Moreover, as Davies (2003: Ch. 7) points out, there is growing realisation that conflict and indiscipline is a direct result of teaching methods, including testing, that encourage competition. Teachers who attempt to motivate pupils by encouraging them to out-perform their peers, and by instilling a fear of doing worse than others, may inadvertently be making them more disruptive. Those who encourage pupils to concentrate on mastering individual tasks are more likely to sustain order and hold the attention of their students. Highly competitive students may deliberately or subconsciously misbehave because they believe that combining being disruptive with getting good grades gives them added value and indicates that they are clever and this is precisely what Clark Pope found in her study in America,

> At times these forms of classroom management required rather aggres-sive behaviour on the part of the students. All but Berto chose to contest a teacher's grading decision during the semester. Kevin regularly voiced dissent over marked errors on tests and quizzes, often resulting in a change of grade . . . With so many students and so many bureaucratic hurdles in the school institution, only the students who made them-selves known, who spoke up and questioned authority got heard. Even if the student's performance did not necessarily warrant an extra point or a higher grade, complaining loudly, strongly and regularly was thought to yield slightly better results, especially since teachers were strapped for time. . . .
>
> (Pope 2001: 152)

Conversely, as Davies (2003) also points out, those at the other end of the scale are equally disruptive because it provides them with a reason for low grades other than low ability. While research in Britain suggests that low-achieving pupils react to competitive testing by becoming demotivated, losing some self-esteem and reducing effort (Henry 2002), in France accord-ing to a UNESCO consultant psychiatrist,

> The aggression some French youngsters show these days isn't a coinci-dence. They're up against a system, focused very much on itself, that doesn't respond to its needs. Education has become hostage to a system where young people have to submit to the rule of competition. This hampers individual performance and growth, in both education and social terms.
>
> (L'homme 2000: 4)

Does the massive apparatus of testing now in place in many educational systems really serve the needs of children or those of the state? All too often the response must be in terms of the latter. The damage that competitive testing is doing to pupils is clear to all who will see. While the selective and stratified basis of higher education and the need for occupational specialisation in the labour market means that qualifications are important to people, the onus should be on the education system to prove why a particular test is deemed necessary. The enormous over-emphasis on testing and grades gets in the way of learning and education and much of it could be scrapped tomorrow not only with no harm to education but also with many positive benefits.

9 Learning to kill
Schooling and militarisation

School is the army for kids. Adults make them go there, and when they get there, adults tell them what to do, bribe and threaten them into doing it, and punish them when they don't.

(John Holt, quoted in Meighan 1994: 10)

Introduction

John Holt's quotation above compares schooling to the military in terms of the element of compulsion and regimented authoritarianism. In many countries he could have added the existence of a standard school 'uniform'. An article on school uniforms in the UK quoted Halla Beloff, a social psychologist at Edinburgh University as arguing that,

We all know deep in our hearts that wearing uniform is a method of control. One of the aims of school is to get you used to the idea of obeying orders and to make you biddable. Sitting in rows, getting there on time, changing activity every 40 minutes, were useful if you were going to be cannon fodder or factory fodder or office fodder. But it isn't so useful these days, when there is more call for creativity.

(*Times Educational Supplement*, Friday 3/10/2003)

Often these uniforms come with insignia of rank such as prefect, monitor or house 'captain' as well as regulated appearance such as length of hair. However, the relationship between the military and schooling is closer than similar organisational forms and symbols. When I was 14 I joined the army because I was at school. All pupils of this age at my school in Britain in the 1960s had to join what was known as the Combined Cadet Force. Once a week we would don military uniforms and practice marching with rifles around the school playing fields. Occasionally we would be taken to the countryside where we would rehearse military tactics of concealment and surprise in order to outwit and kill the enemy. Inside the school was a locked room called the armoury where all the weapons were stored. This puzzled me for years – why was I being trained to kill as part of general academic education? Why did the military have a special relationship with the school curriculum – and why does it still do so?

A key role of the state is to defend its borders and this requires the loyalty of its population. Schooling systems are used by states for purposes of political socialisation and indoctrination and one aspect of this is to create loyalty to the state by encouraging not only obedience and a respect for the authority of the state (or a particular regime) but patriotism and an ability and proclivity to fight for one's country (often portrayed as coterminous with a particular ideology or regime). Thus in some countries such as Prussia/Germany (Green 1990: 32, 130) and Japan (Shipman 1971: Ch. 9) there is a strong historical relationship between schools and the military. In France,

> the strong ties that bind the national education system and the army are as old as compulsory schooling itself. Both institutions served in the building of the nation. Schools served as one of the coloniser's main means of acculturation, enrolling pupils in 1914 to send out letters to the front or to organise fund-raising fairs which helped to maintain hatred and the warlike frenzy of the time. The Second World War saw the Marechal Petain's children trained to sing nationalist songs. (Note: 'Marechal Petain's children' is an expression referring to the children's leagues which developed under the laws of Vichy. Children were trained to sing glory to France and to the collaborationists, racists and anti-semites of the time. They were enrolled, gathered in work camps and learnt the new trilogy of 'Work, Family and Nation'.)
>
> (Mahlen 2001: 15)

Such ties are not just historical, however, and this chapter explores different forms of relationship between the military, violence and schooling both in the recent past and the present.

Military intervention in schooling processes

This is when the military directly intervenes in schooling in order to impose the will of its political masters by force. Southern Africa experienced this form of militarisation during the liberation struggles of the 1970s and 1980s. During the war of independence against South African occupation in Namibia, South African soldiers carried guns while they taught in schools. As one Namibian school pupil put it, 'Imagine somebody teaching you, and if you make a mistake, or if he suspects you, he would just point his gun at you telling you that he would shoot you or your mother' (Konig 1983: 15).

In what was then Rhodesia, the government security forces attempted to frighten schoolchildren into not supporting the liberation forces fighting for an independent Zimbabwe, though the tactic had the opposite effect,

> Parading kids before corpses, or corpses before kids, was common prac-
> tice. It happened in 1976 at Chikore Mission school, 230 kilometres
> south of Umtali, when on three occasions pupils were shown bodies
> which the security forces had brought into the school and dumped in
> the parking lot – genitals exposed, fingers cut off from the knuckles,
> horrifying. Not surprisingly, 140 of the school's 380 pupils responded
> to this treatment by walking across the border into Mozambique in
> July 1976, whereupon the government closed the school and expelled
> five teachers.
>
> (Caute 1983: 59)

In South Africa, the violent suppression of resistance to apartheid took its toll. In the aftermath of the Soweto uprisings the police shot and killed some 1000 students in 1976-7 and many more were injured and arrested (Christie 1991: Ch. 8).

Militarisation of the curriculum

In a range of countries military training has been introduced as part of the school curriculum. In Venezuela, President Chavez decreed in 1999 that all school children would be given military training. The President, a former paratrooper, ruled that children in the 2200 primary and secondary schools must be given lessons in military strategy, weapons handling and national sovereignty issues. President Chavez, who was himself educated in military schools, first announced the militarisation of schools during a four-hour speech to Venezuela's teachers' union. He received a standing ovation when he said that military training would make Venezuela more efficient. President Chavez later said that the military was the only sector of society which had not been tainted by corruption so that it had a lot to teach children – 'Our soldiers will go into schools to teach lessons on war and defence, but also on discipline and national pride' (Gamini 1999). A few months later human rights groups uncovered a series of executions and beatings allegedly carried out by the Venezuelan military in an attempt to stop looting during floods and mudslides that hit Venezuela in December 1999 (Franklin 2000).

In 2000 it was announced in Russia that teenage girls were to be offered military training as part of the school curriculum in the same way as boys. Those girls who receive military training will be listed in the military reserves and will be liable to call-up in times of war. Full combat training would be included as would military theory and practice on the firing range. The extension of military training in schools will allow girls to compete with boys for officer training places at élite military academies, opening up avenues for promotion in the armed services (Louis 2000).

As recently as 1999, in parts of Cambodia still controlled by the Khmer Rouge, children were being taught how to lay landmines, how to set booby traps, how to make weapons from fertiliser and how to transport weapons to the guerrilla fighters on the frontline (Warren 2002a). Comrade Deuch, the chief torturer for the Khmer Rouge during the period of the 'killing fields' between 1975 and 1979 who was responsible for 40,000 deaths, was a former schoolteacher – as indeed was Pol Pot himself. One French citizen imprisoned in Cambodia at this time reports befriending a young girl about the same age as his own daughter while in a prison camp but she was sent away to Khmer Rouge indoctrination classes,

> Gradually her attitude towards the chained Frenchman changed from innocent childish affection to doubt and mistrust. One evening as he lay shackled on the floor, she entered his hut, bent down and inserted her tiny finger between his ankle and the iron links of his chains. Then she skipped away, fetched the key, unlocked the padlock and tightened the chain. This incident explains . . . the unthinking ease with which Khmer Rouge children soldiers, taken from their parents and brainwashed to spy, denounce and kill, were able to execute people without mercy. They were the most powerful and terrifying component of the entire movement.
>
> (Swain 2003)

Davies (1999: 25) describes a newspaper report of 1999 about a Serb school in Kosovo where military training aids were used to instruct children how to use mines and booby traps. Textbooks included diagrams on how to find and attack a tank's weak spots and how to set a mine beneath the ground or in the long grass. The instructions were in Albanian although later reports provided evidence that the instructions had also been found in Serbo-Croat suggesting that both Serb and Albanian children had been taught bomb-making techniques at different periods of the school's history. Davies comments that the 'defence' curriculum is deeply ingrained on both sides.

This has also been the case in Bosnia and Herzegovina where a subject called 'basic civil defence' is part of the curriculum. Among the aims of the subject are,

> 'Give students skills on unarmed and armed defence against an aggressor'
> 'War is our reality, thus to clarify to the students war as a terminology and its characteristics, as well as its consequences for the individual and for the people as a whole'
> 'Teach students first aid and self-defence'

'Create a certainty among students that they can successfully defend themselves independently of the aggressors technological or numerous advantage'
'Teach them how to use a weapon'

Due to external pressures from the international community, education ministers in Bosnia and Herzegovina made an inter-entity agreement in May 2001 to replace this subject with Human Rights and Civic Education but there has been no follow-up evaluation of whether this has been carried out. However, the same article from which this information comes reviewed school textbooks currently in use and concluded that 'the textbooks present human rights and democracy mostly in a negative form i.e. the student is given a negative model of these topics' (Reference to follow – 2003).

In Taiwan in the 1980s,

In every senior school there were military officers (education officers) working under the Department of Discipline. These people supervised our life closely and gave us two hours' military training, or nursing and simply medical training (for girls only) every week. Once a year we were taken to military camps to practise with real guns because of the belief that we might need to defend ourselves anytime. During our school years we had military manoeuvres every year to know where to hide in case of war . . . As the shadow of war was always there, a military influence was very visible in the campus, and remains so today. I remember once a young military officer mentioned that a student living in the dormitory had complained that she had not resealed a letter after reading it. The officer apologised and promised that she would reseal letters next time. Occurrences like these were hardly questioned.

(Chen 2002: 8–9)

In 1972 in South Africa the apartheid regime introduced a subject called 'Youth Preparedness' in the curriculum of white schools. Some of the compulsory parts of the programme included drilling, marching, shooting and self-defence. There was also an emphasis on ceremonies and rituals which prepared children physically for combat and imprinted military attitudes and values (Christie 1991: Ch. 6). Rian Malan, a descendant of one of the main architects of apartheid, recalled that he and others linked the forced regimentation of youth preparedness to the authoritarianism of the wider system,

it made us lob off our sideburns at the earlobe, caned us if we misbehaved and forced us to wear military uniforms on Fridays, when we spent the first hour of the school day marching around the rugby field as part of something called youth preparedness . . . In our eyes there was an unmistakable link between such fascism and the larger workings of apartheid . . .

(Malan 1990: 54–55)

In North Korea primary school children are taught martial songs such as 'Little Tank Rushes Forward' (Watts 2003) while in Libya, school pupils wear a khaki-green uniform and have military training as part of the curriculum, including how to handle a weapon (BBC Radio 4, 2003). In America, the arch-enemy of such rogue states, John Ashcroft, the Attorney General in the Bush Administration, has been linked to a pro-gun lobbying group which believes that the answer to America's school shootings is to allow pupils to be armed in the classroom (Kettle and Martinson 2001). Lynne Cheney, wife of George Bush's deputy, has written a book called *America: A Patriotic Primer* for five-year-olds which has sold very well. The text is set out alphabetically and under 'R is for Rights we are Guaranteed' is the 'Right to Bear Arms' (Sutherland 2002). This emphasis from the Bush administration may be unnecessary as three out of five schoolboys already have easy access to guns and one in five say that they have taken a weapon to school (Borger 2001). Moreover,

> Schools in the American state of Maryland are considering teaching gun safety. Maryland plans to include the subject in health classes, following a one year pilot. Police explained gun safety to children as young as four. Older pupils watched more graphic presentations focusing on the dangers of guns. The state legislature will decide this month whether to make the subject compulsory in school. Other states including California, Texas and Montana have also expressed interest.
>
> (*Times Educational Supplement* 19/1/2001)

Teachers in Utah would be in a good position to help with such classes. In July 2003 they were told that an edict passed in May 2003 permitting them to carry concealed guns in school is not a license to use firearms. They can have the weapons but if they fire them they will be in breach of contract and subject to the law. One board member said 'Some people think they're still in the Wild West', noting that armed police officers already patrol Utah's secondary schools (Phillips 2003b).

In terms of curriculum, it may of course be a matter of what is left out as much as what is included. In Australia,

> Even though, according to UN estimates, some 40 to 50% of scientific research and development since 1945 has been directed to military-related topics, this reality is 'hidden' in high-school physical science and economics textbooks. The problematique of social responsibility in science and technology and the opportunity cost of military related R & D for civilian development and environmental security are ignored

or almost entirely neglected. In physics and chemistry school textbooks, it is rare indeed, for instance, for discussion of nuclear physics to include any mention of the connections between the civilian and military nuclear industries, let alone invite dialogue on the moral dimension of scientific knowledge harnessed for hi-tech weaponry . . . The vast diversion of economic resources to militarism from civilian reconstruction and global ecological security receives scant, if any, treatment in widely used upper secondary economics texts.

(Hutchinson 1996: 52)

In England a science education pack officially approved by the Department of Education and Skills and designed for use by local authority advisers in training sessions for science advisers suggested the following activities: 'Solve problems – make burglar alarm pressure pads, use ball bearings to make tilt switches for bombs etc'. It was later withdrawn (Woodward 2002).

The hidden curriculum

The 'hidden curriculum' refers to everything that is taught and learned in school but which doesn't appear on the overt, planned timetable. Military signals and messages can be transmitted in schooling via means other than the taught curriculum. In Mexico, for example, assemblies and public events in schools have a strong military element to them (Martin 1994). A reporter visiting an Arabic lesson in a Koranic boarding school in Indonesia noted a picture above the classroom of a masked intifada fighter carrying a huge rocket launcher and staring down at a tiny tank. The same school's nature lovers club has as its logo a pair of crossed Kalashnikov automatic rifles (Aglionby 2002).

However, the lessons learnt from the hidden curriculum can be more subtle and indirect in their support of military conflict. In a paper on education and violence in Sierra Leone the author has a section on 'Education as an accomplice to rebellion' in which he argues that the conformity, subservience and blind loyalty fostered by the schooling system have contributed significantly to the military violence between warring factions,

> Even at the height of its academic excellence, education in Sierra Leone tended to produce 'clever conformists' rather than 'daring innovators' . . . [in a school ethos] in which obedient conformity is rewarded, whilst any deviant innovation is punished. Encapsulated in this ethos is a culture of schooling in which teachers know best; school rules exist for the good of pupils and should not be flouted; deference must always be shown to those who 'know better'; respect for those in authority should be maintained at all times; knowledge is there to be acquired, not to be challenged; knowing answers is more important than asking

questions . . . There is a strong reluctance to question authority or deviate from the status quo in most matters. The roots of the sycophancy
problem run deep within the education system.

(Wright 1997: 22)

So that,

Sierra Leoneans can be faulted for acquiescing to suppression and
dictatorship from successive governments because of a fatalist attitude
which borders on fear of freedom. In the midst of gross violations of
human rights, naked corruption and dictatorship, it has never proved
easy to arouse Sierra Leoneans to resist or protest against the powers
that be.

(Wright 1997: 23)

The rebel Revolutionary United Front (RUF) was guilty of carrying out
many atrocities against civilians at the height of the fighting in Sierra
Leone and it is interesting that Wright notes that the RUF had 'an unusually
high proportion of ex-teachers and ex-students in its ranks' (1997: 25).

In Britain the authority structure of schooling is being increasingly
imposed by the ex-military. Former soldiers were hired to work in schools
in Manchester, Merseyside, Leicester, Bristol, the West Midlands and
London. The idea is to cut crime and truancy by giving pupils a 'sense of
responsibility and discipline' (*Times Educational Supplement* 9/3/2001).
Schools in Portsmouth and West Sussex have recruited ex-servicemen to
invigilate exams, supervise classes when teachers are ill or training and
observe colleagues for performance management. A naval resettlement officer was quoted as saying the job 'would be ideal for many ex-servicemen'
(Barnard 2001). Two pilot schemes – one in Norfolk and one in Newcastle
– have been launched which use retired army instructors to help tackle
disaffection, discipline problems and truancy among secondary pupils by
taking them out of school to be involved in a range of different activities.
One of the pupils is quoted as saying 'I used to find lessons boring and
irrelevant but the stuff we learn with the army officers is much more practical and fun' while another said 'We get on with them better than with
the teachers because they speak to us like adults' (Kelly 2001). In another
article on the expansion of the scheme a headteacher was quoted as saying
'The essence of the programme is that the kids are in an environment they
do not associate with normal school and are learning essential skills, such
as working as part of a team, that will help them to get a job when they
leave' (Kelly 2002).

There are two serious issues with these schemes. The first is what they say
about the existing nature of schooling – especially for the pupils left behind.
The second is the *type* of 'order', 'discipline' and 'responsibility' that will be
encouraged and imposed. The military is not, nor necessarily should be,

a democratic organisation. It is a specialised social institution that exists primarily to fight wars. Its authority structure and ethos is hierarchical and authoritarian because that is what is necessary in an organisation that requires immediate obedience and loyalty in order to fight violent battles. So ex-military personnel may well be effective at reinforcing the authoritarian value structures of British schooling as presently constituted but is this what is required? Here we return to Chapter 1 – what should be the goals of education? If a key goal is to be education for democracy, a case that will be argued in the final chapter, then is the military the right organisation to be involved in school discipline and management? Is it likely that it will be in a position to foster *democratic* forms or order, discipline and responsibility required in the wider society?

Recruitment, privileged access to schooling and military normalisation

In some societies the military has privileged and unequal access to schools. One aspect of this is recruitment,

> Israel is a highly militarised country. Society is completely interlocked with the military. Our educational system is such that we gradually groom our children for war. We aid in forming their identity by teaching them to serve in the army.
>
> (Hiller 2002: 19)

> While still at school, Israeli Jewish youths prepare themselves to join the military forces. Lectures are held in school classrooms, delivered by members of the Israeli Defence Force, to give impressions of life in the Israeli army. Some youths volunteer for special units or undergo pre-induction courses.
>
> (Klein 2000: 169)

In France young people between the ages of 16 and 18 have to register with the military authorities and perform what is called a Day's Preparation for the National Fighting Spirit which consists of a day spent having military careers promoted to them. In America the Bush Administration has required headteachers of the 22,000 schools which receive federal funds to give every branch of the armed forces the same access to students as universities and business. As a result of a clause in President Bush's education reform law, schools now have to hand over student names, addresses and phone numbers to military recruiters or face loss of funding. The information gleaned is being used to step up army sales pitches to school-age children, allowing more to be cold-called at home and sent glossy brochures (Phillips 2003c). Parents and teachers in liberal areas have accused the Pentagon of attempting to brainwash children and civil rights organisations say that gathering personal information clearly violates students' privacy (Goldenberg 2002).

These may not be the only issues involved. One writer who works in the Project on Youth and Non-Military Opportunities (YANO) in America makes some interesting potential links between high school shootings and militarisation. In Santana High School, California a 15-year-old, Andy Williams, was accused of killing two people and shooting 13 others in March 2001. The school is located in a very conservative area of San Diego County with close ties to the Klu Klux Klan. San Diego is the location of one of the largest military complexes in the world. Project YANO has regularly attended career fairs at Santana High School to counter the presence of military recruiters. According to the writer of the article, the career fair co-ordinator frequently uses the public address system to encourage students all over campus to visit military exhibits but 'We have never heard her urge them to visit Project YANO'. Santana is one of the very few schools where Project YANO has experienced overt student hostility to its counter-recruitment message. Before Andy Williams packed his gun and left for school in March 2001 he put on a shirt emblazoned with the logo of the US Navy's élite commando unit, the SEALs, and was wearing it when taken into custody. Seventeen days after the Santana incident another student at another school brought in two guns and wounded six people. He told police that he intended to shoot a school administrator who had been responsible for the US Navy rejecting his enlistment a day earlier. Traits common to the perpetrators of rage shootings in US schools are a sense of victimisation, prejudice and an interest in the military. The article concludes,

> There is a profound irony in schools being attacked by students fascinated with the military. As primary instruments for socialisation and the teaching of values, educational institutions in the US have, for the last decade, been the main focus of efforts by the military to extend its domestic influence. The armed forces have been expanding high school military training programmes and developing new ones geared for lower school levels. In addition, official partnerships between individual military units and schools are increasingly being established to facilitate student tours of military bases and classroom visits by uniformed personnel. Retired aircraft carriers and battleships are being converted into floating war museums, to which entire school student bodies are being brought for propagandising. These various efforts, along with aggressive military recruiting activities and the more general intrusion of militarism in the culture (via movies, music, computer games and the general media) are further popularising military values and soldiering among young people. In any country where the military is allowed to have such a powerful presence in the educational system, there

should be little surprise if even a relatively few decide to respond to the pressures of life by resorting to mass violence. Our behaviour is motivated in large part by our values and it is inevitable that the strong influence of militarism on those values is going to come out in such a way.

(Jahnkow 2001: 29)

In Britain an article appeared just after the war in Iraq in May 2003 which described how an infants' school had a number of teddy bears that parents and teachers take with them on trips abroad and photograph 'in exotic locations' with local children for later use with British children in school. One bear had been taken to Iraq by one of the fathers fighting in the war and there is a picture of the teddy bear sitting on a trench with three soldiers. The whole tone of the article is that the parent who went to Iraq was simply on another trip to an exotic location. The idea that this trip was qualitatively different in intention and purpose from going on holiday is not mentioned (Thornton 2003). A cuddly teddy bear being used to symbolise a very controversial war in which many people lost their lives, or at least bits of their bodies, some would argue needlessly, is another example of how military values can become normalised and accepted as uncontroversial in schools.

Teacher education

Finally, military training and learning to kill can also be a part of in-service teacher education. A newspaper article on a 'reorientation camp' for teachers in Zimbabwe in early 2003 began,

> The title of the first lesson was Patriotism. It began with raised-fist salutes and chanted slogans in praise of 'Great Leader Robert Mugabe' and ended with denunciation of Britain's Prime Minister. 'Tony Blair is a pig and we don't want to associate with the pig and his gay classmates' the class was told. Later they learnt how to strangle enemies of the state with their shoelaces.
>
> (Lamb 2003)

The idea is to get to the younger generation through indoctrinating teachers. Teachers are afraid not to attend because refusal is taken as meaning support for the opposition. Apart from being subjected to crude propaganda, teachers in the camps reported using a textbook called 'Book of Fallen Heroes' which included heroes such as the man behind the violent invasions of white-owned farms and the man who set up training camps for ZANU youth militia known as Green Bombers responsible for a number of atrocities. One teacher said, 'they showed us how to kill someone by striking them on the back of the neck just behind the ear with a heavy object and to strangle them with shoelaces so you wouldn't be detected' (Lamb 2003). At the end of such camps teachers are given a Certificate of National Service, and job adverts for teachers now state 'Preference will be given to National Service graduates'. The same teacher, who had run away and hidden, said, 'I had been proud to be a teacher, I wanted to educate children, to be a source of enlightenment but now it's all spoilt. The whole education system is destroyed' (Lamb 2003).

Conclusion

I am not a pacifist. I don't believe that war is never justified. Moreover, I have a brother who is a senior officer in the armed forces and I am very proud of him. However, the military is by definition a violent institution in that it exists essentially to fight wars even if sometimes it has to take on humanitarian roles. It ought to be a specialised and professional institution that trains only its selected personnel. Educational organisations may well discuss issues of war and violence but the aim should be to stress the need for peaceful conflict resolution or management wherever and whenever possible. War should not be regarded as the norm in education, the military should not have privileged access to schools above other organisations and military training should certainly not be part of the curriculum. Education needs to have as its top priority a framework for the development of democratic and peaceful individuals and societies and this is the subject of the final chapter.

10 Education for democracy and peace

People die for democracy, go to prison for democracy, send their children to fight in wars for democracy, and yet we fail to educate our children for democracy. We need to educate for democracy.

(Estelle Morris, former British Secretary of State for Education and Skills, in *The International Young Citizen's College*, brochure advertising University of the First Age, Birmingham)

Examples of violence towards pupils by schools are disturbingly easy to come by if one chooses to look and see. It would be good if in the future politicians, academics and others concerned with educational policy always acknowledged in their speeches and their writing that schools do harm as well as good and that school–pupil violence exists as well as pupil–teacher and pupil–pupil violence. The problem must be openly acknowledged and confronted. Then schools should be stopped from doing harm. According to the UN Convention on the Rights of the Child, which most countries signed up to in 1989, it is the responsibility of the state to protect the child from violence, injury or abuse. So schools must stop harming children in the ways that have been described.

However, I want to end the book by moving beyond this to look at what education ought to do – what sort of education should we be striving for? The place to begin is with the goals of education. What is it we are trying to achieve at a fundamental level? What sort of people and what sort of society? Everything else should flow from this. Answers to questions concerning the improvement of education like 'better examination results', or 'better behaved pupils' or 'more effective schools' beg more questions than they answer as they tell you nothing about the philosophical and ideological context which is needed to judge words like 'better', 'examination', 'behaviour' and 'effective'.

For the writer, the twin fundamental goals of education should be both peace and democracy which in my view cannot be separated. The achievement of more peaceful societies also requires the institutionalisation of greater levels of democracy than is currently the case globally. Democracy provides the best political environment available for the peaceful solution of disputes and conflicts. Authoritarian regimes, usually military or single party, have been marked by civil unrest, violent repression and resistance, over-high levels of military expenditure and wars against neighbours. This has caused enormous damage to the economies of countries and severely affected their social fabric. It is also one major reason why authoritarian government has been a serious obstacle to international efforts at poverty reduction (Harber 2002a). While democracies are far from being perfect, accountable and representative government minimises internal violence and greatly decreases the possibility of going to war without good reason, though it doesn't guarantee it. At the micro level of social institutions such as the workplace or the school, if they are organised democratically then there is an emphasis on the peaceful solution of problems and disagreements through discussion and participation rather than imposition, confrontation, conflict and violence.

However, democracy is not possible without democrats. Democracy is only sustainable in a supportive political culture where a sufficient proportion of the population has a high commitment to democratic values, skills and, particularly, behaviours. This is based on an understanding of democracy that goes beyond the minimum ritual of voting (or not voting) every four or five years in an election. While democracy does require an informed citizenry capable of making genuine political choices, it also requires a fuller and deeper notion of democracy that forms the basis of a democratic *society* in which people actually behave in a democratic manner in their daily interactions. Democracy is not genetic, it is learned behaviour. There is nothing in our genes to programme us as democrats or dictators at birth. Therefore education must have a clear idea of the sort of democratic person it hopes to cultivate. What are the characteristics of such a person? Somebody described as democratic would, for example, celebrate social and political diversity, work for and practice mutual respect between individuals and groups, regard all people as having equal social and political rights as human beings, respect evidence in forming their own opinions and respect the opinions of others based on evidence, be open to changing one's mind in the light of new evidence and possess a critical and analytical stance towards information. The democratic citizen would possess a proclivity to reason, open-mindedness and fairness and the practice of co-operation, bargaining, compromise and accommodation.

If education is to help to foster and develop such characteristics, then its organisation should reflect democracy in its daily practices as democratic values and behaviours are learned as much by experience as by hearing or reading about them. Education must offer opportunities for democratic participation and for the learning of democratic political skills and values in practice in terms of institutional and curriculum organisation. Despite the existence of mounting evidence that democratic schools are more effective than conventional schools in a range of ways (e.g. Harber 1997b;

Trafford 1997, 2003), contemporary formal schooling is an authoritarian experience for many and a violent, damaging and dehumanising experience for some. Power and authority over what is learned, when, where and how is not with learners and, in many cases, not even with teachers. This is despite article 12 of the UN Convention on the Rights of the Child which says that children have the right to express an opinion, and to have that opinion taken into account, in any matter or procedure affecting the child. Modern mass schooling systems are not on the whole contributing to the development of more democratic and peaceful individuals and societies and indeed were not primarily designed to do so in the first place. However, it is important not to advocate the replacement of one orthodox form of educational provision with another. There is no single, perfect means of organising learning. Any system or vehicle of provision of education can be used for good (in my view that means democratic) or bad (authoritarian and potentially violent) purposes. What is important are the purposes and practices of education.

The main concern of the present book is with schooling as violence. Education for peace and democracy could be a book in its own right and indeed has been on many occasions. What follows here then is a necessarily selective and short review of some existing published literature on education for democracy and the peaceful settlement of conflicts at a series of levels and in a series of contexts plus some interesting specific examples of interventions aimed at democracy and peace. The international examples used in this literature review have been chosen because they discuss real attempts at fostering democratic forms of education rather than being purely theoretical debates about, or prescriptive recommendations for, democratic education and education for peace, though many do contain theory and prescription as well. A number of the positive examples presented exist in states where there are also negative examples that have been described in the previous chapters demonstrating yet again the contested and contradictory nature of educational theory and practice.

Global initiatives

UNESCO's Associated Schools Project Network has existed for fifty years and now contains over 7000 schools in 170 countries. A key purpose of this network is the fostering of peace and democracy through education. Survey evidence from the schools themselves, Ministry of Education officials and ASPnet national coordinators on the operation of the network (Davies *et al.* 2003) found that, while there were exceptions and in some contexts the network was not as robust as it might be, nevertheless the overwhelming majority saw schools in the network as distinctive from other schools in their emphasis on peace, democracy, open-mindedness and internationalism. Interestingly 'quality', an ambiguous term much used in educational debates, was defined in terms of respect for diversity, peace and human rights work, student democracy and active learning and teaching methods. Many concrete examples were given to support these statements. Examples and discussion of how the ASPnet works to promote democracy in a range of countries (Costa Rica, France, Hungary, Senegal, Switzerland, Colombia and the Philippines) can be found in Meyer-Bisch (1995). Project Gemini is an online global citizenship project supported by the British Department for Education and Skills and the Department for International Development. Schools in Britain are linked with schools in India and South Africa and do research and have discussions on topics like the Israeli/Palestinian conflict in the Middle East. This has enabled pupils not only to learn about the Middle East but also to find out about each other's cultures, to express opinions and to be tolerant of the views of others (Cole 2003).

System reform

Some countries have consciously designed their formal education systems to foster democracy for some time. Research by Davies and Kirkpatrick (2000) demonstrates how educational policy in Germany, Denmark, Sweden and The Netherlands has been designed to support and develop democracy. There is firm and wide-ranging legislation to ensure that pupils are involved in decision making. There are also laws and rules on pupils being involved in the planning of curricula and teaching. Pupil councils often had a special room in the school with a computer and telephone where they could network and produce reports and newsletters. School student unions were well established and active regional and national systems of pupil representation meant that pupil associations, or education committees with pupils on them, were routinely consulted by government whenever educational change was proposed. Pupils could also lobby for educational improvement. Relationships between pupils and teachers were mainly warm, respectful and non-confrontational. Pupils felt that they could give their opinions and that teachers listened to them. Pupils could define democracy, knew about human rights and knew how to create change if necessary.

In South Africa a significant policy change in education was signalled after the first democratic elections in 1994 with the 1995 *White Paper on Education and Training* which said that,

> The realisation of democracy, liberty, equality, justice and peace are necessarily conditions for the full pursuit and enjoyment of lifelong learning. It should be a goal for education and training policy to enable a democratic, free, equal, just and peaceful society to take root and prosper in our land, on the basis that all South Africans without exception share the same inalienable rights, equal citizenship and common destiny, and that all forms of bias (especially racial, ethnic and gender) are dehumanising.
>
> (Department of Education 1995: 22)

In 2001 the South African Department of Education produced the *Manifesto on Values, Education and Democracy*. This document provides an important example of an attempt to set all education in the country within a coherent philosophical framework. In many ways it is the mirror opposite of education under apartheid or in Nazi Germany. In these two cases the entire education system was geared to reproducing a very negative and violent ideology. The Manifesto attempts to tease out what education for democracy actually means for a wide range of aspects of educational practice so that it informs and provides an ultimate reference point for all educational debates. Whether it be maths education, teaching methods or school management – how can, should or does it contribute to building democracy? The Manifesto talks of, 'moulding a people from diverse origins, cultural practices, languages, into one, within a framework democratic in character, that can absorb, accommodate and mediate conflicts and adversarial interests without oppression and injustice' (Department of Education 2001: I).

In post-apartheid South Africa there is considerable clarity at the policy level about the ultimate democratic purposes and goals of curriculum, management and access and such a document would be useful in any national context. The reality in South African schools is often very different of course, as we have seen in this book and which is discussed in more detail elsewhere (Harber 2001a). South African formal education still has a long way to go to actually achieve the goals set out in the Manifesto but at least the signposts are clear. Neighbouring Namibia has also been in the process of developing policy to democratise its education system (Harber 1997a: Ch. 9; Angula and Grant-Lewis 1997; Avenstrup 1998) and in Colombia the Escuela Nueva or New School Movement attempted to introduce more democratic forms of teaching and learning in rural primary schools. By 1991 some 20,000 of the country's 27,000 rural primary schools were involved (Harber and Davies 1997: Ch. 9). In the Czech Republic, 56 schools are involved in piloting a reform aimed at abolishing the national curriculum in favour of learning targets. The idea is to use flexible, child-centred methods where the pupils are as much part of the teaching process as the staff. According to one teacher involved in the pilot, the approach results in 'self-confident children, not afraid to question authority, who know how to find and process information' (Holdsworth 2002).

In terms of peace education, examples of systemic efforts in an American state and in sub-Saharan Africa can be found in Harris (1996). In Cambodia, an example used negatively in the chapter on militarisation, books about the regime of the Khmer Rouge are now being introduced into schools for the first time. The Director of the Documentation Centre of Cambodia, who spent seven years compiling evidence of the genocide, stated that 'Without additional learning tools, children can become mirrors of their parents. We must learn to ask questions of our history. . . . Many of today's children can't believe it happened'. They cannot accept that children killed their parents in their own country (Warren 2002b). In Albania education about guns and gangsters is now part of the curriculum as part of mines and weapons awareness education aimed at teaching children that guns are dangerous both to themselves and to society. The scheme is funded by UNICEF and attempts to 'deglamorise' guns in a country where there is widespread access to weaponry (Moszynski 2000). In Palestine, government officials responsible for reforming school books and the curriculum have begun to phase out anti-Israeli and anti-semitic material. While children are nevertheless exposed to the violent conflict, the books aim to lower the levels of emotions by removing exaggerations (Ward 2003b). In Cyprus, teachers unions in the northern, Turkish part of the island have recently called on Greek and Turkish education officials to eliminate racism and extreme nationalism from school syllabuses in both parts of the island. The unions want a joint committee that will examine aspects of the curriculum that 'provoke fanaticism and confrontation' (Morgan 2003).

Individual schools

Individual schools have also consistently tried to operate in a more demo-cratic manner within educational systems that haven't necessarily encouraged it. Some of these schools have been state schools and some have operated in the private sector. Many have been deliberately planned as small schools in order to facilitate more human and less anonymous forms of relationship. Examples from Britain and America are described and discussed in Harber and Meighan (1989); Carnie (2003: Ch. 5); Harber (1996 – including an example from Israel); Ayers, Klonsky and Lyon (2000); Apple and Beane (1999) and Trafford (1997). While many of these sources also make reference to creating democratic classrooms, Beyer (1996) specifically covers this topic in relation to America. Jensen and Walker (1989) and Davies and Kirkpatrick (2000) contain examples from a range of European countries while Harber (1998a, b) has examples from southern Africa. An interesting case study of involving school pupils in research into democratic education in Chile is provided in Fielding and Prieto (2002). Schooling is, of course, not synonymous with education. Meighan (1997) reviews evidence that suggests that home-based education can also make an important contribution to the democratic forms of learning.

In terms of education for peace or non-violence, there are now many books and manuals on creating a safer school, often using techniques like peer mediation to facilitate non-violent conflict resolution in schools. Here the purpose is to present some example case studies of how schools can be made to be less violent places and actively contribute to peace. One example of such is a study by Harber (2001b) which discusses research on a project in three schools in South Africa. One key theme of this project was the need for schools to create a more inclusive, democratic environment in order to foster a climate of openness and a sense of ownership, commitment and responsibility. In the midst of a civil war, some schools in Colombia maintain this emphasis on democracy with elected councils, peace conflict resolution groups and an emphasis on human relations between staff and pupils. In one region of Colombia, the regional policy and strategy co-ordinator for the region notes that, 'In Latin America we tend to think that children aren't worth listening to, so their voices aren't heard and their rights are ignored'. However, she states this in the context of supporting a particular school where pupils are actively involved in the government of the school. One pupil said 'It is very different from my old school. The pupils don't punish you – they give you advice. You have to work with every-one else and respect others'. The hope is that increased education of this sort would help reduce recruitment to the warring armed groups and, as one teacher puts it, 'we'll have kids who are more creative, less fearful and less submissive. They won't blindly follow orders and they'll be less likely to go to war' (Hodgson 2003: 8–9). In Jerusalem in a wider context of inter-communal intolerance, a school opened in 1998 that aims at bilingual and bicultural education for both Jewish and Arab pupils. Its key aim is the pro-motion of coexistence and partnership. It was founded by Israelis of Arab and Jewish origin and is staffed by teachers who work in pairs, teaching sequentially in Hebrew and Arabic. All religious and political holidays are observed and the customs and food of Arabs, Jews and Christians are cele-brated, enabling the children to share each other's culture (Ward 2003c).

Teacher education

Teacher education has been characterised by the 'myth of the liberal college' – that is the myth that there is a contradiction between the liberal, pro-gressive and democratic college or university on the one hand and the traditional, conservative and authoritarian school on the other. This myth suggests that student teachers are exposed to the more radical, democratic forms of teaching and learning during their courses in higher education but are rapidly re-socialised into more authoritarian understandings and prac-tices during their teaching practice and their subsequent employment in education. Rather than there being a contradiction between the two, in terms of power over what is taught and learned, how and when, teacher education is often an authoritarian preparation for teaching in schools (Harber 1994). Recent interviews with initial teacher training students carried out by the writer in England and South Africa tend to confirm the 'do as I say' rather than 'do as I do' nature of initial teacher education. Examples of attempts to change teacher education to reflect democratic values and practice are not particularly easy to come by though concrete examples from Britain and Africa are discussed in Harber (1997a, 1994) and from in-service teacher education in South America and Africa in Shaeffer

(1990). A research project which sought to develop knowledge and skills among teacher educators in The Gambia is discussed in Schweisfurth (2002b). Education for Reconciliation is a cross-border programme in the Republic of Ireland and Northern Ireland that trains teachers to use collaborative work in dealing with the sectarian preconceptions surrounding the lives of pupils. Use is made of citizenship education to raise and deal with emotionally charged issues in a democratic manner in order to foster non-violent conflict resolution (Klein 2003).

Conclusion

Formal education is, and always has been, a site of struggle between differing views about the nature of humanity and desirable forms of social organisation. Most of this book has discussed the widespread occurrence of authoritarian forms of schooling as a means of social control leading in some cases – far too many cases – to violence against pupils and the perpetuation and perpetration of violence in the wider society. In the view of the writer, however, the examples used in the final chapter of this book represent hope. There is nothing fixed or immutable about the nature of schooling. Schooling is socially and political constructed and can be reconstructed as these examples show. This is not necessarily an easy or comfortable task as the weight of tradition, dominant ideology, perceived 'common sense' and vested interests often have to be challenged and overcome. These issues cannot and should not be avoided by all those involved in education. The issue of schooling as violence has certainly not been given the systematic international attention it deserves. Avoiding these questions and focusing solely on 'technical' problems simply means reproducing systems as they presently are. In many cases this is both foolhardy and dangerous. Education can be more democratic and geared to the promotion of the peaceful settlement of conflict as this chapter has illustrated. Nothing in education is more important than this.

References

Abello, M. (1997) 'Are the seeds of violence sown in schools?', *Prospects* XXVII: 447–465.

Adams, R. (1991) *Protests By Pupils: Empowerment, Schooling and the State* (London: Falmer Press).

Advisory Group on Citizenship (1998) *Education for Citizenship and the Teaching of Democracy in Schools* (The Crick Report) (London: Qualifications and Curriculum Authority).

Aglionby, J. (2002) 'Writing on the wall for "terror school"', *Guardian* 22/10.

Alexander, R. (2000) *Culture and Pedagogy: International Comparisons in Primary Education* (Oxford: Blackwell).

Alibhai-Brown, Y. (2000) 'Be at ease in your own skin', *Times Educational Supplement* 12/5.

Altbach, P. and Kelly, G. (1978) *Education and Colonialism* (London: Longman).

Anderson, J. (1991) 'Death of the Dinosaurs?', in P. Toogood (ed.), *Small Schools* (Ticknall: Education Now).

Anderson, S. and Payne, M. (1994) 'Corporal punishment in elementary education: views of Barbadian schoolchildren', *Child Abuse and Neglect* 18(4): 377–386.

Angula, N. and Grant Lewis, S. (1997) 'Promoting democratic processes in educational decision making: reflections from Namibia's first five years', *International Journal of Educational Development* 17(3): 233–249.

Apple, M. (2001) *Educating the 'Right' Way* (London: RoutledgeFalmer).

Apple, M. and Beane, J. (1999) *Democratic Schools: Lessons from the Chalkface* (Buckingham: Open University Press).

Avenstrup, R. (1998) 'The democratisation of education in post-apartheid Namibia', in C. Harber (ed.), *Voices for Democracy: A North–South Dialogue on Education for Sustainable Democracy* (Nottingham: Education Now in association with the British Council).

Ayers, W. (2000) 'Simple justice: thinking about teaching and learning, equity, and the fight for small schools', in W. Ayers, M. Klonsky and G. Lyon (eds), *A Simple Justice: The Challenge of Small Schools* (New York: Teachers College Press).

Ayers, W., Klonsky, M. and Lyon, G. (eds) (2000) *A Simple Justice: The Challenge of Small Schools* (New York: Teachers College Press).

Azevedo, M. (1980) 'A century of colonial education in Mozambique', in A. T. Mugomba and M. Nyaggah (eds), *Independence Without Freedom* (Santa Barbara: ABC-Clio).

Badran, A. (ed.) (1989) *At the Crossroads: Education in the Middle East* (New York: Paragon House).

Balegamire, J. B. (1999) 'Children, children's rights and the context of their education in South Kivu in the Democratic Republic of the Congo', *Prospects* XXIX(2): 246–258.

Baranovic, B. (2001) 'History textbooks in post-war Bosnia', *Intercultural Education* 12(1): 13–26.

Barnard, N. (2001) 'How to soldier on in a shortage', *Times Educational Supplement* 27/4.

Barnes, B. (1982) 'Education for socialism in Mozambique', *Comparative Education Review* 26(3): 406–419.

Barnett, E., de Koning, K. and Francis, V. (1995) *Health and HIV/AIDS Education in Primary and Secondary Schools in Africa and Asia* (London: Overseas Development Administration).

Bates, S. (2000a) 'Educating Gita', *Guardian* 14/3.

Bates, S. (2000b) 'Anger at growing textbook bias in India', *Guardian* 25/1.

Bauer, C. (1996) 'The lofty redbrick tradition', *Sunday Times* (Durban) 23/6.

BBC Radio 4 (2003) 'Crossing continents – Libya' broadcast 1/5.

Behal, S. (2000) 'Exam stress prompts reform demand', *Times Educational Supplement* 21/7.

Behal, S. (2001a) 'Beaten for saying "Good Morning"', *Times Educational Supplement* 30/3.

Behal, S. (2001b) 'Head tried to sell pupils for vice trade', *Times Educational Supplement* 22/6.

Behal, S. (2002a) 'Rebellion in Delhi over biased history texts', *Times Educational Supplement* 18/10.

Behal, S. (2002b) 'Exercise in discipline kills girl', *Times Educational Supplement* 12/7.

Behal, S. (2002c) 'Caste cruelty makes school a nightmare', *Times Educational Supplement* 26/4 .

Behal, S. (2003) 'Just an hour of homework – at age three', *Times Educational Supplement* 9/5.

Benbenishty, R. and Astor, R. A. (2003) 'Violence in schools: the view from Israel', in P. Smith (ed.), *Violence in Schools: the Response in Europe* (London: RoutledgeFalmer).

Benn, R. (2000) 'The genesis of active citizenship in the learning society', *Studies in the Education of Adults* 32(2): 241–256.

Berliner, W. (2001) 'Gay in silence', *Education Guardian* 2/10.

Berliner, W. (2003) 'Testing, testing', *Education Guardian* 29/4.

Bernal, E. C. (1997) 'Colombia: country and schools in conflict', in *Final Report and Case Studies on the Workshop on Educational Destruction and Reconstruction in Disrupted Societies* (Geneva: International Bureau of Education and the University of Geneva).

Beyer, L. (1996) *Creating Democratic Classrooms* (New York: Teachers College Press).

Biddulph, S. (1998) *Raising Boys* (London: Thorsons).

Biggs, J. (1996) 'Western misconceptions of the Confucian heritage learning culture', in D. Watkins and J. Biggs (eds), *The Chinese Learner: Cultural, Psychological and Contextual Influences* (Hong Kong: Comparative Education Research Centre).

Birkett, D. (2001) 'The school we'd like', *Education Guardian* 5/6.

Black, I. (2002) 'EU defies critics to extend sanctions on Harare elite', *Guardian* 23/7.

Block, A. (1997) *I'm Only Bleeding: Education as the Practice of Social Violence against Children* (New York: Peter Lang).

Borger, J. (2001) 'Gun culture still fills US schools', *Guardian* 3/4.

Borger, J. (2002) 'Saddam, tell me about your mum', *Guardian* 14/11.

Bosely, S. (2002) 'Aids epidemic "bringing social collapse" ', *Guardian* 27/11.

Bourne, R., Gungara, J., Dev, A., Ratsoma, M., Rukanda, M., Smith, A. and Birthistle, U. (1998) *School-Based Understanding of Human Rights in Four Countries: A Commonwealth Study* (London: Department for International Development).

Bowles, S. (1976) 'Cuban education and revolutionary ideology', in P. and G. Figueroa (eds), *Sociology of Education: A Caribbean Reader* (Oxford: Oxford University Press).

Bowles, S. and Gintis, H. (1976) *Schooling in Capitalist America* (London: Routledge and Kegan Paul).

Bray, M. and Lee, W. (2001) *Education and Political Transition: Themes and Experiences in East Asia* (Hong Kong: Comparative Education Research Centre, University of Hong Kong).

Bright, M. (2000) 'Revealed: why evil lurks in us all', *Observer* 17/12.

Broadfoot, P. (1999) 'Comparative research on pupil achievement: in search of validity, reliability and utility', in R. Alexander, P. Broadfoot and D. Phillips (eds), *Learning from Comparing, Vol. 1* (Oxford: Symposium Books).

Broadfoot, P. (2000) 'Assessment and Intuition', in T. Atkinson and G. Claxton (eds), *The Intuitive Practitioner* (Buckingham: Open University Press).

Brooks, K. (2000) 'Studying for a future', *Times Educational Supplement Friday*, 9/6.

Burke, J. (2000) 'Children suffer stress over their "love lives" ', *Observer* 29/10.

Bush, K. and Saltarelli, D. (eds) (2000) *The Two Faces of Education in Ethnic Conflict* (Florence: UNICEF).

Campos, B. P. (1991) 'Psychological development and personal and social education in schools', in H. Starkey (ed.), *Socialisation of School Children and their Education for Democratic Values and Human Rights* (Amsterdam: Swets and Zeitlinger).

Cardoso, C. M. N. (1998) 'The colonialist view of African-origin "Other" in Portuguese society and its education system', *Race, Ethnicity and Education* 1(2): 191–206.

Carnie, F. (2003) *Alternative Approaches to Education* (London: RoutledgeFalmer).

Carr, W. and Hartnett, A. (1996) *Education and the Struggle for Democracy* (London: Cassell).

Carroll, R. (2000) 'Right seeks to vet "textbook wrongs" ', *Guardian* 13/11.

Carroll, R. (2002) 'The Eton of Africa', *Guardian* 25/11.

Carter, C., Harber, C. and Serf, J. (2003) *Towards Ubuntu: Critical Teacher Education for Democratic Citizenship in South Africa and England* (Birmingham: Birmingham Development Education Centre).

Carvel, J. (2000) 'Parents call for schools to bring back the cane', *Guardian* 8/1.

Carvel, J. (2002) 'Better education making us nation of liberals', *Guardian* 4/12.

Casely-Hayford, L. (1999) *Education, Culture and Development in Northern Ghana: Micro Realities and Macro Context: Implications for Policy and Practice* (unpublished PhD thesis, University of Sussex).

Caute, D. (1983) *Under the Skin* (Harmondsworth: Penguin).

Chen, I-Ru (2002) *Democratisation, Gender and School Leadership in Taiwan* (unpublished PhD thesis, University of London).

Christie, P. (1991) *The Right to Learn* (Johannesburg: SACHED/Ravan).

Codjoe, H. M. (2001) 'Fighting a public enemy of Black academic achievement – the persistence of racism and the schooling experiences of Black students in Canada', *Race, Ethnicity and Education* 4(4): 343–375.

Colclough, C. with Lewin, K. (1993) *Educating All the Children: Strategies for Primary Schooling in the South* (Oxford: Clarendon Press).

Cole, G. (2003) 'Blessed are the peacemakers', *Education Guardian* 23/9.

Connell, R. (2000) 'Arms and the man: using the new research on masculinity to understand violence and promote peace in the contemporary world', in I. Breines, R. Connell and I. Eide (eds), *Male Roles, Masculinities and Violence* (Paris: UNESCO).

Cosgrove, J. (2000) *Breakdown: The Facts About Stress in Teaching* (London: RoutledgeFalmer).

Crighton, J. (2000) 'Learning among the ruins: schooling and ethnic strife' (unpublished paper delivered at informal seminar, University of Warwick, March).

Cullingford, C. (2000) *Prejudice: From Individual Identity to Nationalism in Young People* (London: Kogan Page).

Davies, I., Gregory, I. and Riley, S. (1999) *Good Citizenship and Educational Provision* (London: Falmer Press).

Davies, L. (1993) 'Teachers as implementers or subversives', *International Journal of Educational Development* 8(4): 293–304.

Davies, L. (1994) *Beyond Authoritarian School Management* (Ticknall: Education Now).

Davies, L. (1999) *Education in Kosova: Report to the British Council* (unpublished paper, University of Birmingham).

Davies, L. (2003) *Education and Conflict: The Edge of Chaos* (London: Routledge-Falmer).

Davies, L. and Kirkpatrick, G. (2000) *The EURIDEM Project: A Review of Pupil Democracy in Europe* (London: Children's Rights Alliance).

Davies, L., Harber, C. and Schweisfurth, M. (2003) *Global Review of ASPnet* (Paris: UNESCO).

Dawson, R., Prewitt, K. and Dawson, K. (1977) *Political Socialisation* (Boston: Little, Brown).

Dean, K. A., Hartmann, P. and Katzen, M. (1983) *History in Black and White* (Paris: UNESCO).

Department of Education (South Africa) (1995) *White Paper on Education and Training* (Pretoria).

Department of Education (South Africa) (2001) *Manifesto on Values, Education and Democracy* (Pretoria).

Devine, J. (1996) *Maximum Security: The Culture of Violence in Inner-City Schools* (Chicago: University of Chicago Press).

Dneprov, E. (1995) 'Background to the reform and new policies in Russia', in J. Chapman, I. Froumin and D. Aspin (eds), *Creating and Managing the Democratic School* (London: Falmer Press).

Dunn, S. and Morgan, V. (1999) 'A fraught path – education as a basis for developing improved community relations in Northern Ireland', *Oxford Review of Education* 25(1) and (2): 141–154.

Dutter, B. (1997) 'One third of Britons admit to racism and xenophobia', *Weekly Telegraph* 24–30 December.

Dyanti, A. (1999) 'No sex education, please . . . teachers walk out of Aids lecture', *Saturday Star* (Johannesburg) 31/7.

East, J. (2001) 'Reformers say parrots not welcome', *Times Educational Supplement* 29/6.

Elbedour, S., Center, B., Maruyama, G. and Assor, A. (1997) 'Physical and psychological maltreatment in schools', *School Psychology International* 18: 201–215.

Ellis, A. (1985) *Educating Our Masters: Influences on the Growth of Literacy in Victorian Working Class Children* (Aldershot: Gower Publishing Company).

Esteve, J. (2000) 'The transformation of the teacher's role at the end of the twentieth century: new challenges for the future', *Educational Review* 52(2): 197–208.

Fagerlind, I. and Saha, L. (1989) *Education and National Development*, 2nd edn (Oxford: Pergamon Press).

Farah, I. and Bacchus, K. (1999) 'Educating girls in Pakistan: tensions between economics and culture', in F. Leach and A. Little (eds), *Education, Cultures, and Economics: Dilemmas for Development* (London: RoutledgeFalmer).

Farrell, M. (2003) 'Racism exposed in secondaries', *Times Educational Supplement* 26/9.

Fasheh, M. (1999) 'Learning versus development: a Palestininan perspective', in F. Leach and A. Little (eds), *Education, Cultures, and Economics: Dilemmas for Development* (London: RoutledgeFalmer).

Fielding, M. and Prieto, M. (2002) 'The central place of student voice in democratic renewal: a Chilean case study', in M. Schweisfurth, L. Davies and C. Harber *Learning Democracy and Citizenship* (Oxford: Symposium).

Fife, W. (1997) 'The importance of fieldwork: anthropology and education in Papua New Guinea', in M. Crossley and G. Vulliamy (eds), *Qualitative Educational Research in Developing Countries* (New York: Garland).

Fitzpatrick, M. (2000) 'Alarm at surge in abuse by teachers', *Times Educational Supplement* 17/11.

Fitzpatrick, M. (2001) 'Parents of bullied boy win record payout', *Times Educational Supplement* 2/2.

Fitzpatrick, M. (2002) 'National pride to be compulsory', *Times Educational Supplement* 1/11.

Fitzpatrick, M. (2003) 'Earthquake drill will not save pupils in decrepit buildings', *Times Educational Supplement* 7/3.

Foucault, M. (1977) *Discipline and Punish* (London: Penguin Books).

Fox, C. (1999) 'Girls and women in education and training in Papua New Guinea', in C. Heward and S. Bunwaree (eds), *Gender, Education and Development* (London: Zed Books).

Frank, B. (1996) 'Masculinities and schooling: the making of men', in Ross Epp and A. Watkinson (eds), *Systemic Violence: How Schools Hurt Children* (London: Falmer Press).

Franklin, J. (2000) 'Army accused of killings during Venezuela's floods', *Guardian* 15/1.

Freire, P. (1972) *Pedagogy of the Oppressed* (London: Sheed and Ward).

Fullan, M. (1991) *The New Meaning of Educational Change* (London: Cassell).

Fuller, B. (1991) *Growing Up Modern* (London: Routledge).

Galtung, J. (1981) 'The specific contribution of peace research to the study of violence: typologies', in UNESCO, *Violence and Its Causes* (Paris: UNESCO).

Gamini, G. (1999) 'Guns in school draw ovation', *Times Educational Supplement* 9/7.

Ginott, H. (1972) *Teacher and Child* (New York: Macmillan).

Giroux, H. (1986) 'The politics of schooling and culture', *Orbit* 17(4): 10–11.

Goffe, L. (2003) 'Abused gays find refuge in school of their own', *Times Educational Supplement* 8/8.

Goldenberg, S. (2001) 'Class war', *Education Guardian* 31/7.

Goldenberg, S. (2002) 'Parents furious as Pentagon slides recruiting officers into classrooms', *Guardian* 5/12.

Goodlad, J. (1984) *A Place Called School* (New York: McGraw Hill).

Gorvett, J. (2000) 'Conflict leaves scarred pupils', *Times Educational Supplement* 15/9.

Gorvett, J. (2001) 'Turkey: girl pupils face virginity testing', *Times Educational Supplement* 20/7 (www. tes. co. uk).

Gourevitch, P. (1998) *We Wish to Inform You that Tomorrow We Will be Killed with Our Families* (New York: Farrar, Strauss and Giroux).

Gramsci, A. (1977) *Selections from the Prison Notebooks of Antonio Gramsci*, Q. Hoare and G. Nowell Smith (ed. and trans.) (London: Lawrence and Wishart).

Green, A. (1990) *Education and State Formation* (London: Macmillan).

Green, D. (1998) *Hidden Lives: Voices of Children in Latin America and the Caribbean* (London: Cassell).

Greenfield, N. (2000) 'Schools let the abusers hunt on', *Times Educational Supplement* 21/4.

Greenfield, N. (2002) 'School failed to stop gay bullying', *Times Educational Supplement* 19/4.

Grenfell, M. and James, D. (1998) *Bourdieu and Education* (London: Falmer Press).

Griffith, R. (2000) *National Curriculum: National Disaster?* (London: Routledge-Falmer).

Gulbenkian Foundation (1995) *Children and Violence* (London: Calouste Gulbenkian Foundation).

Hackett, G. (2001) 'The most over-tested nation in the world', *Times Educational Supplement* 27/4.

Hallam, R. (1994–5) 'Sexual harassment, sex education and teenage pregnancy', *African Woman* June 1994 to February 1995.

Handy, C. (1984) *Taken for Granted? Understanding Schools as Organisations* (York: Longman).

Hanuki, H. (2000) 'The current state of Japanese children's human rights' (unpublished seminar paper, University of Birmingham).

Harber, C. (1987) *Political Education in Britain* (Lewes: Falmer Press).

Harber, C. (1989) *Politics in African Education* (London: Macmillan).

Harber, C. (1991) 'International contexts for political education', *Educational Review* 43(3): 245–256.

Harber, C. (1992) *Democratic Learning and Learning Democracy* (Ticknall: Education Now).

Harber, C. (1994) 'International political development and democratic teacher education', *Educational Review* 46(2): 159–166.

Harber, C. (1996) *Small Schools and Democratic Practice* (Nottingham: Educational Heretics Press).

Harber, C. (1997a) *Education, Democracy and Political Development in Africa* (Brighton: Sussex Academic Press).

Harber, C. (1997b) 'International developments and the rise of education for democracy', *Compare* 27(2): 179–191.

Harber, C. (1998a) 'Desegregation, racial conflict and education for democracy in South Africa', *International Review of Education* 44: 569–582.

Harber, C. (ed.) (1998b) *Voices For Democracy* (Nottingham: Education Now).

Harber, C. (2001a) *State of Transition: Post-Apartheid Educational Reform in South Africa* (Oxford: Symposium Books).

Harber, C. (2001b) 'Schooling and violence in South Africa: creating a safer school', *Intercultural Education* 12(3): 261–271.

Harber, C. (2002a) 'Not quite the revolution: citizenship education in England', in L. Davies, C. Harber and M. Schweisfurth (eds), *Learning Democracy and Citizenship: International Experiences* (Oxford: Symposium Books).

Harber, C. (2002b) 'Education, democracy and poverty reduction in Africa', *Comparative Education* 38(3): 267–276.

Harber, C. and Dadey, A. (1991) *Training and Professional Support for Headship in Africa* (London: Commonwealth Secretariat).

Harber, C. and Davies, L. (1997) *School Management and Effectiveness in Developing Countries* (London: Cassell).

Harber, C. and Meighan, R. (1989) *The Democratic School* (Ticknall: Education Now).

Harding, L. (2002) 'A vision of hell in Indian city gorging on violence', *Guardian* 2/3.

Harris, B. (2001) 'Trouble as a bad time', *Times Educational Supplement* 1/6.

Harris, I. (1996) 'Peace Education in a Postmodern World', *Peabody Journal of Education* 71(3): 63–83.

Hedges, J. (2002) *Becoming a Teacher in Ghana: A Qualitative Study of Newly Qualified Teachers in Central Region, Ghana* (unpublished PhD thesis, University of Sussex).

Hemming, J. (1991) 'Size matters', in P. Toogood (ed.), *Small Schools* (Ticknall: Education Now).

Henry, J. (2002) 'Constant examining demotivates low achievers', *Times Educational Supplement* 28/6.

Heyneman, S. and Todoric-Bebic, S. (2000) 'A renewed sense for the purposes of schooling: the challenges of education and social cohesion in Asia, Africa, Latin America, Europe and Central Asia', *Prospects* XXX(2): 145–166.

Hiller, R. (2002) 'Chipping away at the core', *Peace News* June–August: 19.

Hodgson, M. (2003) 'Learning after the conflict': I 'Taking children seriously' (London: *Guardian*/Save the Children).

Holdsworth, N. (2002) 'Targets herald new era of reform', *Times Educational Supplement* 15/11.

Holmes, M. and Wynne, E. (1989) *Making the School an Effective Community* (Lewes: Falmer).

Holt, J. (1969) *How Children Fail* (Harmondsworth: Penguin).

Holt, J. (1982) *Teach Your Own* (Brightlingsea: Lighthouse Books).

Holt, J. (1991*) Learning All the Time* (Ticknell: Education Now).

Houndoumadi, A. and Peteraki, L. (2001) 'Bullying and bullies in Greek elementary schools: pupils' attitudes and teachers'/parents' awareness', *Educational Review* 53(1): 19–26.

House, R. (2000) 'Stress, surveillance and modernity', *Education Now News and Review* 30, Winter.

Human Rights Watch (1999a) *Spare the Child: Corporal Punishment in Kenyan Schools* (Washington: Human Rights Watch).

Human Rights Watch (1999b) *Broken People: Caste Violence Against India's 'Untouchables'* (New York: Human Rights Watch).

Human Rights Watch (2001) *Scared at School: Sexual Violence Against Girls in South African Schools* (New York: Human Rights Watch).

Hutchinson, F. (1996) *Educating Beyond Violent Futures* (London: Routledge).

Ichilov, O. (1990) *Political Socialisation, Citizenship Education and Democracy* (New York: Teachers College Press).

Ideus, K. (1994) 'Cultural foundations of ADHD: a sociological perspective', *Therapeutic Care and Education* 3(2): 173–192.

IJED (1996) Special edition of the *International Journal of Educational Development* on the World Bank and Structural Adjustment.

Illich, I. (1971) *Deschooling Society* (Harmondsworth: Penguin).

Jahnkow, R. (2001) 'School violence: a result of bad parenting or militarism', *Peace News* September–November: 28–29.

Jennings-Wray, Z. D. (1984) 'Implementing the integrated approach to learning: implications for integration of the curricula of primary schools in the Caribbean', *International Journal of Educational Development* 4(4): 265–278.

Jensen, K. and Walker, S. (1989) *Towards Democratic Schooling: European Experiences* (Milton Keynes: Open University Press).

Jones, C. (1985) 'Sexual tyranny: male violence in a mixed secondary school', in G. Weiner (ed.), *Just a Bunch of Girls* (Milton Keynes: Open University Press).

Jones, J. (1994) 'Towards an understanding of power relationships in institutional abuse', *Early Child Development and Care* 100: 69–76.

Juma, M. (2001) *Coping with HIV/AIDS in Education* (London: Commonwealth Secretariat).

Juon, H.-S., Nam, J. and Ensminger, M. (1994) 'Epidemiology of suicidal behaviour among Korean adolescents', *Journal of Child Psychology* 35(4): 663–676.

Kai-ming, C. (1997) 'Qualitative research and educational policy-making: approaching reality in developing countries', in M. Crossley and G. Vulliamy, *Qualitative Educational Research in Developing Countries* (New York: Garland Publishing).

Kang, S-W. (2002) 'Democracy and human rights education in South Korea', *Comparative Education* 38(3): 315–326.

Katz, A., Buchanan, A. and Bream, V. (2001) *Bullying in Britain: Testimonies from Teenagers* (East Molesey: Young Voice).

Kawaguchi, A. (2000) 'The rights of the child and education in Japan in the light of the United Nations Convention', *Prospects* XXX(4): 497–508.

Kelly, A. V. (1986) *Knowledge and Curriculum Planning* (London: Harper and Row).

Kelly, A. (2000) 'Heads outperform captains of industry', *Times Educational Supplement* 18/12.

Kelly, A. (2001) 'Corps curriculum fires up teen spirit', *Times Educational Supplement* 16/3.

Kelly, A. (2002) 'Drafted into war on truancy', *Times Educational Supplement* 5/7.

Kenway, J. and Fitzclarence, L. (1997) 'Maculinity, violence and schooling: challenging poisonous pedagogies', *Gender and Education* 9(1): 117–133.

Kettle, M. and Martinson, J. (2001) 'Bush's choice linked to "Guns for Pupils" group', *Guardian* 13/1.

Kigotho, W. (2001) 'Unrest sparks call for cane', *Times Educational Supplement* 24/8.

Kigotho, W. (2002) 'Strike breakers caned in classroom', *Times Educational Supplement* 4/10.

King, N., Ollendick, T., Murphy, G. and Molloy, G. (1998) 'Utility of relaxation training with children in school settings: a plea for realistic goal setting and evaluation', *British Journal of Educational Psychology* 68: 53–66.

Kirkman. S. (2003) 'Sick and tired of tests', *Times Educational Supplement* 28/3.

Klein, R. (1999) *Defying Disaffection* (London: Trentham Books).

Klein, R. (2000) 'Teacher-trainees bullied', *Times Educational Supplement* 15/9.

Klein, R. (2003) 'Take the troubles', *Times Educational Supplement, Respect* 4/7.

Klein, U. (2000) 'Our best boys: the making of masculinity in Israeli society', in I. Breines, R. Connell and I. Eide (eds), *Male Roles, Masculinities and Violence* (Paris: UNESCO).

Klonsky, M. (2000) 'Remembering Port Huron', in W. Ayers, M. Klonsky and G. Lyon (eds), *A Simple Justice: The Challenge of Small Schools* (New York: Teachers College Press).

Ko, J.-H. and Apple, M. (1999) 'Teachers, politics and democracy: the Korean teachers and educational workers union and the struggle for independence', *Education and Social Justice* 2(1): 67–73.

Kohn, A. (1993) *Punished by Rewards* (Boston: Houghton Mifflin).

Konig, B. (1983) *Namibia: The Rages of War* (London: International Defence and Aid Fund for Southern Africa).

Kundani, H. (1999) 'States of mind', *Guardian Higher* 16/11.

Lamb, C. (2003) 'Mugabe bends minds in hatred campaign', *The Sunday Times* 9/2.

Landry, B. (1997) 'Education in a multicultural society', in P. Hall (ed.), *Race, Ethnicity and Multiculturalism* (New York: Garland Publishing).

Leach, F. (2001) 'Conspiracy of silence? Stamping out abuse in African schools', *Insights Development Research* August.

Leach, F. (2002) 'Learning to be violent – the role of the school in developing adolescent gendered identity' (paper presented at the conference of the British Association of International and Comparative Education, University of Nottingham).

Leidig, M. (2000) 'Big Brother tracker has children in sight', *Times Educational Supplement* 1/12.

Leonardos, A. (1993) 'CIEP: A democratic school model for educating economically disadvantaged students in Brazil?', in H. Levin and M. Lockheed (eds), *Effective Schools in Developing Countries* (London: Falmer Press).

Levin, H. M. (1987) 'Work and education', in G. Psacharopoulos (ed.), *Economics of Education: Research and Studies* (Oxford: Pergamon).

Levine, R. (1963) 'Political socialisation and cultural change', in C. Geertz (ed.), *Old Societies and New States* (New York: The Free Press).

L'homme, C. (2000) 'The violence they live with', UNESCO *Sources* No. 126.

Lindsey, U. (2003) 'Spate of suicides sparks call to ease exam pressure', *Times Educational Supplement* 15/8.

Lockheed, M. (1993) 'The condition of primary education in developing countries', in H. Levin and M. Lockheed (eds), *Effective Schools in Developing Countries* (London: Falmer Press).

London, N. (2002) 'Curriculum convergence: an ethno-historical investigation into schooling in Trinidad and Tobago', *Comparative Education* 38(1): 53–72.

Loomba, A. (1998) *Colonialism/Postcolonialism* (London: Routledge).

Louis, J. (2000) 'Russia lets slip the girls of war', *Times Educational Supplement* 11/2.

Lucas, B. (2000) 'Towards a learning age', *Guardian* 14/3.

MacDonald, I. (1996) 'Expanding the lens: student perceptions of school violence', in J. Ross Epp and A. Watkinson (eds), *Systemic Violence: How Schools Hurt Children* (London: Falmer Press).

McGreal, C. (2002) 'Gay claims force out Mugabe's TV chief', *Guardian* 4/4.

MacGregor, K. (2000) 'Teachers in terror over attacks', *Times Educational Supplement* 30/6.

McGurk, H. (1987) *What Next?* (London: Social and Economic Research Council).

McKay, V. (1995) *A Sociology of Educating* (Johannesburg: Lexicon Publishers).

Mahlen, M. (2001) 'Civic duty?', *Peace News* September–November: 15.

Mahoney, P. (1985) 'A can of worms: the sexual harassment of girls by boys', in P. Mahoney, *Schools for the Boys?* (London: Hutchinson).

Malan, R. (1990) *My Traitor's Heart* (London: Vintage).

Maloney, K. (1997) '25% of KZN schools are dangerous', *The Mercury* (Durban) 23/5.

Mama, A. (2000) 'Transformation thwarted: gender-based violence in Africa's new democracies', *African Gender Newsletter*, University of Cape Town, 6: 1–3.

Mangan, J. A. (ed.) (1993) *The Imperial Curriculum: Racial Images and Education in the British Colonial Experience* (London: Routledge).

Mansell, W. (2002) 'Teachers blamed over gay bullying', *Times Educational Supplement* 6/12.

Mansell, W. and Bloom, A. (2002) 'Tests turn toddlers into "battery hens"', *Times Educational Supplement* 27/9.

Mansour, S. (1996) 'The Intifada generation in the schoolroom', *Prospects* XXVI(2): 293–310.

Marshall, J. (2000) 'Teenage killings fuel wave of anxiety', *Times Educational Supplement* 15/12.

Marshall, J. (2001) 'Cover-up over pupil abuse', *Times Educational Supplement* 23/2.

Marshall, J. (2003) 'Alarm over an epidemic of ennui', *Times Educational Supplement* 24/1.

Martin, C. (1994) *Schooling in Mexico* (Aldershot: Avebury).

Masien, G. (2003) 'Countrywide action to stop the bullies', *Times Educational Supplement* 14/11.

Mason, A. and Palmer, A. (1996) *Queer Bashing* (London: Stonewall).

Massialas, B. and Jarrar, S. (1991) *Arab Education in Transition: A Source Book* (New York: Garland).

Mbilinyi, M. J. (1979) 'Secondary education', in H. Hinzen and V. H. Hundsdorfer (eds), *The Tanzanian Experience* (London: Evans).

Meehan, M. (1999) 'Israeli textbooks promoting hatred of Palestinians', *Washington Report on Middle East Affairs* (http: //www. wrmea. com).

Meighan, R. (1992) *Learning from Home-Based Education* (Ticknall: Education Now).

Meighan, R. (1994) *The Freethinkers' Guide to the Educational Universe* (Nottingham: Educational Heretics Press).

Meighan, R. (1997) *The Next Learning System* (Nottingham: Educational Heretics Press).

Meighan, R. (1999) 'Compulsory mass schooling as an infringement of human rights', *Human Rights Education Newsletter* 23: 4.

Meighan, R. and Siraj-Blatchford, I. (1997) *A Sociology of Educating*, 3rd edn (London: Cassell).

Meldrum, A. (2002) 'Mugabe repays his foes with starvation', *Guardian* 25/7.

Meyer, B. (1984) 'Knowledge and culture in the Middle East: some critical reflections', in K. Watson (ed.), *Dependence and Independence in Education: International Perspectives* (Beckenham: Croom Helm).

Meyer, B. (1988) 'Moral education in Taiwan', *Comparative Education Review* 32: 20–38.

Meyer-Bisch, P. (1995) *Culture of Democracy: A Challenge for Schools* (Paris: UNESCO).

Milgram, S. (1971) *Obedience to Authority* (London: Tavistock).

Miller, A. (1987) *For Your Own Good* (London: Virago).

Mirembe, R. (2002) 'AIDS and democratic education in Uganda', *Comparative Education* 38(3): 291–302.

Mirembe, R. and Davies, L. (2001) 'Is schooling a risk? Gender, power relations and school culture in Uganda', *Gender and Education* 13(4): 401–416.

Mollayev, A. (2003) 'Fire safety probe as 50 children die in a week', *Times Education Supplement* 18/4.

Molteno, M., Ogadhoh, K., Cain, E. and Crumpton, B. (2000) *Towards Responsive Schools: Supporting Better Schooling for Disadvantaged Children* (London: Department for International Development/Save the Children).

Moore, L. (2002) 'Scared, not skiving', *Guardian Education* (8/1).

Morgan, T. (2003) 'Too-long division', *Times Educational Supplement, Respect* (special supplement).

Morrell, R. (1998) 'Gender and education: the place of masculinity in South African schools', *South African Journal of Education* 18: 218–225.

Morrell, R. (1999) 'Beating corporal punishment: race, masculinity and educational discipline in the schools of Durban, South Africa (paper presented at the Voices in Gender and Education Conference, University of Warwick, March).

Morris, P. and Cogan, J. (2001) 'A comparative overview: civic education across six societies', *International Journal of Educational Research* 35: 109–123.

Moszynski, P. (2000) 'Albania to bring guns into class', *Times Educational Supplement* 14/4.

Motala, S., Vally, S. and Modiba, M. (1999) 'A call to action: a review of minister K. Asmal's educational priorities', *Quarterly Review of Education and Training in South Africa* 6(3): 1–34.

Moumouni, A. (1968) *Education in Africa* (London: Andre Deutsch).

Mshengu, S. and the Midlands Women's Group (2003) 'Ngiyahhala – I am crying', *Children First* 7(49): 18–21.

Nagel, T. (1992) *Quality Between Tradition and Modernity: Patterns of Communication and Cognition in Teacher Education in Zimbabwe* (Oslo: University of Oslo Pedagogisk Forskningsintitutt).

Najcevska, M. (2000) 'Education, masculinity and violence', in I. Breines, R. Connell and I. Eide (eds), *Male Roles, Masculinities and Violence* (Paris: UNESCO).

Newbold, D. (2002) 'Nation searches rubble for answers', *Times Educational Supplement* 8/11.

Newbold, D. (2003) 'Inquiry into tragic school collapse', *Times Educational Supplement* 10/1.

Nieuwenhuys, O. (1994) *Children's Lifeworlds: Gender, Welfare and Labour in the Developing World* (London: Routledge).

Nissan, E. (1996) *Sri Lanka: A Bitter Harvest* (London: Minority Rights Group).

Nyerere, J. (1967) *Education for Self-Reliance* (Dar Es Salaam: The Government Printer).

O'Kane, M. (2000) 'Children of genocide', *Guardian* 21/12.

Omale, J. (2000) 'Tested to the limit', in J. Mirsky and M. Radlett (eds), *No Paradise Yet* (London: PANOS/Zed).

O'Moore, M. and Minton, S. (2003) 'Tackling violence in schools: a report from Ireland', in P. Smith (ed.), *Violence in Schools: The Response in Europe* (London: RoutledgeFalmer).

Oshako, T. (ed.) (1997) *Violence at School: Global Issues and Interventions* (Paris: UNESCO).

Palme, M. (1997) 'Teaching hieroglyphs with authority', in M. John (ed.), *A Charge Against Society: The Child's Right to Protection* (London: Jessica Kingsley).

Parker-Jenkins, M. (1999) *Sparing the Rod: Schools, Discipline and Children's Rights* (Stoke on Trent: Trentham).

Pasalic-Kreso, A. (1999) 'Education in Bosnia and Herzegovina: minority inclusion and majority rules', *Current Issues in Comparative Education* 2(1): 1–9.

Phillips, S. (2003a) 'Kindergartens told to test', *Times Educational Supplement* 31/1.

Phillips, S. (2003b) 'Teachers with guns warned they are not in the Wild West', *Times Educational Supplement* 1/8.

Phillips, S. (2003c) 'Let in the army or risk your funding', *Times Educational Supplement* 11/7.

Pillay, C. (2000) 'Call for AIDS impact study', *The Mercury* 20/4.

Pope, D. C. (2001) *Doing School: How We Are Creating a Generation of Stressed Out, Materialistic and Miseducated Students* (New Haven: Yale University Press).

Porteous, K. (1999) *Youth Violence in Schools* (Pretoria: Secretariat for Safety/ Department of Education and National Youth Commission).

Postman, N. and Weingartner, C. (1969) *Teaching as a Subversive Activity* (Harmondsworth: Penguin).

Pring, R. (1984) *Personal and Social Education in the Curriculum* (London: Hodder and Stoughton).

Prophet, R. and Rowell, P. (1990) 'Curriculum in action: the "practical" dimension in Botswana classrooms', *International Journal of Educational Development* 10(1): 17–26.

Prunier, G. (1995) *The Rwanda Crisis of 1959–1994: History of a Genocide* (London: Hurst and Company).

Purpel, D. E. (1989) *The Moral and Spiritual Crisis in Education: A Curriculum for Justice and Compassion in Education* (Massachusetts: Bergin and Bergin).

Rayner, J. (2001) 'The hidden truth behind race crime in Britain', *Observer* 18/2.

Reimer, E. (1971) *School is dead: An Essay on Alternatives in Education* (Harmondsworth: Penguin).

Reimers, F. (1994) 'Education and structural adjustment in Latin America and sub-Saharan Africa', *International Journal of Educational Development* 14(2): 119–130.

Retamal, G. and Aedo-Richmond, R. (eds) (1998) *Education as a Humanitarian Response* (London: Cassell).

Revell, P. (2002) 'Where's school sonny?', *Education Guardian* 11/6.

Riley, K. and Docking, J. (2002) 'Perceptions of schooling among disadvantaged pupils' (paper delivered to the British Educational Research Association, Exeter, September).

Roland, E. and Munthe, E. (1989) *Bullying: An International Perspective* (London: David Fulton).

Ross Epp, J. (1996) 'Schools, complicity and sources of violence', in J. Ross Epp and A. Watkinson (eds), *Systemic Violence: How Schools Hurt Children* (London: Falmer Press).

Rousmaniere, K., Dehli, K. and de Coninck-Smith, N. (1997) *Discipline, Moral Regulation and Schooling* (New York: Garland).

Ruiz, R. O. (1998) 'Indiscipline or violence? The problem of bullying in school', *Prospects* XVIII(4): 587–599.

Russell, J. (2003) 'It's the Old School tedium that holds children back', *Sunday Times* 26/1.

Salisbury, J. and Jackson, D. (1996) *Challenging Macho Values* (London: Falmer Press).

Salmi, J. (1999) 'Violence, democracy and education: an analytic framework' (paper delivered to the Oxford International Conference on Education and Development, September).

Samoff, J. (1994) *Coping with Crisis: Austerity, Adjustment and Human Resources* (London: Cassell).

Samoff, J. (1999) 'Institutionalising international influence', in R. Arnove and C. Torres (eds), *Comparative Education: The Dialectic of the Global and the Local* (Oxford: Rowman and Littlefield).

Santhiram, R. (1995) 'Friendship patterns in multi-racial schools: with special reference to a minority community in Malaysia', *International Journal of Educational Development* 15(2): 165–174.

Scherrer, C. (2002) *Genocide and Crisis in Central Africa: Conflict Roots, Mass Violence and Regional War* (Westport: Praeger).

Schostack, J. (1986) *Schooling the Violent Imagination* (London: Routledge and Kegan Paul).

Schweisfurth, M. (2002a) *Teachers, Democratisation and Educational Reform in Russia and South Africa* (Oxford: Symposium Books).

Schweisfurth, M. (2002b) 'Democracy and teacher education: negotiating practice in The Gambia', *Comparative Education* 38(2): 303–314.

Searle, C. (1981) *We're Building the New School!* (London: Zed Press).

Serpell, R. (1993) *The Significance of Schooling: Life Journeys in an African Society* (Cambridge: Cambridge University Press).

Sey, P. (2000) *Culture, Democracy and School Effectiveness: A Study of Gambian Primary Schools* (unpublished PhD thesis, University of Birmingham).

Shaeffer, S. (1990) 'Participatory approaches to teacher training', in V. Rust and P. Dalin (eds), *Teachers and Teaching in the Developing World* (New York: Garland).

Sharma, Y. (2001a) 'Nazis win over tenth of pupils', *Times Educational Supplement* 16/3.

Sharma, Y. (2001b) 'Primary pupils turn to stress pills', *Times Educational Supplement* 13/7.

Shaw, M. (2003) 'Keeping tags on safety', *Times Educational Supplement* 12/9.

Shaw, M. and Ormston, M. (2001) 'Values and vodka: a cross-cultural anatomy of an Anglo-Russian educational project', *International Journal of Educational Development* 21: 119–133.

Shipman, M. (1971) *Education and Modernisation* (London: Faber).

Shumba, A. (2001) ' "Who guards the guards in schools?" A study of reported cases of child abuse by teachers in Zimbabwean secondary schools', *Sex Education* 1(1): 77–86.

Shute, C. (1992) *Compulsory Schooling Disease* (Nottingham: Educational Heretics Press).

Simon, B. (1994) *The State and Educational Change* (London: Lawrence and Wishart).

Skelton, A. (1993) 'On becoming a male physical education teacher: the informal culture of students and the construction of hegemonic masculinity', *Gender and Education* 5: 289–303.

Skinner, J. (2001) 'Teachers who abuse: the impact on school communities', *Educational Research* 43(2): 161–174.

Smith, H. (2002) 'Island dream', *Education Guardian* 29/1.

Smith, P. (ed.) (2003) *Violence in Schools: The Response in Europe* (London: RoutledgeFalmer).

Smithers, R. (2000a) 'Blunkett launches anti-bully guidelines', *Guardian* 11/12.

Smithers, R. (2000b) 'Exams regime harms pupils', *Guardian* 4/8.

South African Department of Education (2000) *Guidelines for Alternatives to Corporal Punishment* (Pretoria: Department of Education).

Spelvins, K. (2002) 'Girls at risk from sex abuse by teachers', *Times Educational Supplement* 29/11.

Spyrou, S. (2002) 'Images of "the Other": "the Turk" in Greek Cypriot children's imaginations', *Race, Ethnicity and Education* 5(3): 255–272.

Stacey, B. (1978) *Political Socialisation in Western Society* (London: Edward Arnold).

Stewart, W. (2003) 'Scared to meet the head in the corridor', *Times Educational Supplement* 11/4.

Strauss, M. (1994) *Beating the Devil out of Them* (New York: Lexington Books).

Sullivan, K. (1996) 'Japan tries school uniforms for teachers', *Guardian Weekly* 31/3.

Surnoor, H. and Behal, S. (1998) 'Call for punishment ban', *Times Educational Supplement* 22/5.

Sutherland, J. (2002) 'How to stop student liberalism in the US: get to them when they're five', *Guardian* 10/6.

Swain, J. (2003) 'Witness to the executions', *Sunday Times Magazine* 26/1.

Tabulawa, R. (1995) *Culture and Classroom Practice: A Socio-Cultural Analysis of Geography Classrooms in Botswana Secondary Schools and Implications for Pedagogical Change* (unpublished PhD thesis, University of Birmingham).

Tafa, E. (2002) 'Corporal punishment: the brutal face of Botswana's authoritarian schools', *Educational Review* 54(1): 17–26.

Thornton, K. (2000) 'Bullies thrive in staffroom', *Times Educational Supplement* 18/2.

Thornton, K. (2003) 'Meet Diddy the where bear', *Times Educational Supplement* 23/5.

Toffler, A. (1970) *Future Shock* (London: Bodley Head).

Trafford, B. (1997) *Participation, Power-Sharing and School Improvement* (Nottingham: Educational Heretics Press).

Trafford, B. (2003) *School Councils, School Democracy, School Improvement* (Leicester: Secondary Heads Association).

Troyna, B. (1993) *Racism and Education* (Buckingham: Open University Press).

Tshoane, M. (2001) 'Strangers in their own territory: searching for a path in a complex terrain', *Quarterly Review of Education and Training in South Africa* 8(3): 1–24.

UNDP (2001) *Human Development Report* (Oxford: Oxford University Press).

UNESCO (1989) *Seville Statement on Violence*, www. unesco. org/human_rights/ hrfv.htm

UNESCO (2002) *Education for All: Is the World on Track?* (Paris: UNESCO).

UNESCO (2003) *Education Today* No. 4, January–March.

UNICEF (2001) 'Children in war', http://www. unicef.org/children-in-war/

USAID (2003) *Unsafe Schools: A Review of School-Related Gender-Based Violence in Developing Countries* (Washington: USAID).

Usher, R. and Edwards, R. (1994) *Postmodernism and Education* (London: Routledge).

Vally, S. (2000) 'Reassessing policy and reviewing implementation: a maligned or misaligned system?', *Quarterly Review of Education and Training in South Africa* 7(2): 1–35.

Vally, S. (2001) 'Fundamentalism and the fundamentals of education', *Quarterly Review of Education and Training in South Africa* 8(4): 1–39.

Vally, S. and Dalamba, Y. (1999) *Racism, 'Racial Integration' and Desegregation in South African Public Secondary Schools* (Johannesburg: South African Human Rights Commission).

Van Der Werf, G., Creemers, B., De Jong, R. and Klaver, E. (2000) 'Evaluation of school improvement through an educational effectiveness model: the case of Indonesia's PEQIP project', *Comparative Education Review* 44(3): 329–355.

Velloso, A. (1998) 'Peace and human rights in the Middle East: comparing Jewish and Palestinian experiences', *International Review of Education* 44(4): 257–378.

Villegas-Reimers, E. (1993) 'Where do we go from here?', *Colloquium on Education for Democracy: Proceedings of a Workshop* (Washington DC: USAID).

Walker, D. (2002) 'Education may be the key to extremist actions', *Guardian* 29/7.

Ward, H. (2002) 'Children forced out of sick beds', *Times Educational Supplement* 27/9.

Ward, H. (2003a) 'Infants in test distress', *Times Educational Supplement* 25/4.

Ward, O. (2003b) 'History textbooks try to foster harmony in traumatised town', *Times Educational Supplement* 23/5.

Ward, O. (2003c) 'Friendships amid fear', *Times Educational Supplement* 4/7.

Ward, H., Henry, J. and Mansell, W. (2002) 'Tests swallow up whole year', *Times Educational Supplement* 1/11.

Warren, M. (2002a) 'After the terror', *Times Educational Supplement* 4/1.

Warren, M. (2002b) 'Children to learn about the Khmer Rouge', *Times Educational Supplement* 3/5.

Watkins, K. (1999) *Education Now: Break the Cycle of Poverty* (Oxford: Oxfam).

Watson, K. (1982) 'Education and colonialism in peninsular Malaysia', in K. Watson (ed.), *Education in the Third World* (Beckenham: Croom Helm).

Watts, J. (2003) 'Daily drills, nightly blackouts: North Korea is certain it's next on the US list', *Guardian* 7/2.

West, D. (2000) 'Ban on the use of the cane', *Times Educational Supplement* 27/10.

WHO (World Health Organization) (2002) *World Report on Violence and Health* (Geneva: WHO).

Wiggs, T. (2000) 'Brutal lessons on need for rights', *Times Educational Supplement* 8/9.

Willan, P. (2002) 'Earthquake school built on the cheap', *Guardian* 2/11.

Williams, C. (2001) 'Big Brother is watching too', *Times Educational Supplement* 8/6.

Williams, E. (2003) 'Exams', *Times Educational Supplement Friday* 28/3.

Williams, H. (2003) 'Cheaper than the police', *Guardian* 23/7.

Willis, P. (1977) *Learning to Labour* (Farnborough: Saxon House).

Wolpe, A.-M., Quinlan, O. and Martinez, L. (1997) *Gender Equity in Education: Report of the Gender Equity Task Team* (Pretoria: Department of Education).

Woodward, W. (2000) 'Learning, United', *Education Guardian* 19/12.

Woodward, W. (2002) 'How science lessons could go down a bomb', *Guardian* 27/11.

Woodward, W. (2003) 'Schools tests breach UN convention, envoy claims', *Guardian* 14/7.

Wright, C. (1997) 'Reflections on Sierra Leone: a case study', in *Final Report and Case Studies of the Workshop on Educational Destruction and Reconstruction in Disrupted Societies* (Paris: UNESCO).

Young, S. (2002) 'The barber, the farmer and an African dream', *Times Educational Supplement Friday* 18/10.

Zimmer, J. (1992) 'Asia: diary of a community educator', in C. Poster and J. Zimmer (eds), *Community Education in the Third World* (London: Routledge).

Index